## About the Author

A proud Lancashire lass, I love to meet people and travel to new places. I love shoes, shopping and holidays in the sun. I like to think I've got a good sense of humour, but my husband thinks I'm mad!

# Dedication

*Writing a book has been a desire of mine for many years and admittedly, I did actually start this quite some time ago but a series of events in my life, of which you will become aware as you read on, forced me to put the pen to rest for a while. I did make a promise to myself that I would resume only when I knew in my heart that the time was right for me to do so. That time is now. If it has reached just one reader who can associate with any of its content in any way at all I will feel I have, at the very least achieved something, but if I have helped or encouraged anyone about facing a personal, difficult, or as in my own situation, a life changing decision, then I will have achieved greatly.*

*I would like to dedicate this book to the man who really made all this possible, who turned my life around, who helped me to find myself again and show me what happiness and living but more importantly, love and all it truly means, and that is My Darling Husband, friend and soul mate Mark! I love you with all my heart for all you have done for me, all that you do with me and for everything we share together. I have never been so happy or felt so adored, loved and fulfilled in my entire life. Thank you.*

*Eternally yours*
*Sue*

## SUE ASHLEY

# ALL MY TOMORROWS

AUSTIN MACAULEY
PUBLISHERS LTD.

A CIP catalogue record for this title is available from the British Library.

ISBN 9781786297051 (Paperback)
ISBN 9781786297068 (Hardback)
ISBN 9781786297075 (eBook)

www.austinmacauley.com

First Published (2017)
Austin Macauley Publishers Ltd.
25 Canada Square
Canary Wharf
London
E14 5LB

# Acknowledgments

I should like to say thank you anyone who has read this book (should anyone be so kind as to take the time). I should also like to say thank you especially to Mark for coming into my life and turning it round, I hadn't realised how much of life I had missed until he showed me.

A very special thank you goes to my dearest sister, Diane, whom whilst I was writing this was diagnosed with cancer, who so bravely suffered its presence and has thankfully fought it off with her strength and determination. She also has proof read and approved of my work and words. I have brought back many memories for her, too, that we have since re-lived together through tears of both sadness and joy. Thank you, Diane. I shall be here for you whenever you need me; I love you. Last, but certainly not least, to my wonderful friend and daughter Sarah-Jane, I love you to the moon and back.

# CHAPTER ONE

I was the youngest of four children, and was born in 1960. It was immediately following my difficult and possibly life-threatening birth for both mum and me that it was confirmed to my mother that there would not be a fifth child. Having two brothers and a sister has had its moments and I have many happy memories. However, it was certainly not the case that *this* youngest child was spoilt and had an easy life.

We were a close, happy family, at least this was my belief in my early years, but over time, there developed a great barrier between myself and George, my older brother of ten years. His hard and eccentric behaviour worsened over time, making my life quite unbearable at times. It became apparent even from my earliest memories that he really did seem to harbour some great resentment towards me. I don't know to this very day why this was the case and I only wish I did, as it would perhaps answer some of the many unanswered questions in my mind. He frequently displayed signs of extreme jealousy, as a result of which he mentally and physically abused me. They were dreadful experiences that I can never forget.

Phillip was the next eldest, being eight years older than me and things could not have been more different between the two of us. He was my hero. Fun, considerate and gentle in nature (unlike George), Phillip would often jump in to protect his little sister, whether from George or anyone else who threatened me in any way. Whomever it was they would learn the hard way, as he was quite a force to be reckoned with when it came to my protection! Whether I wanted him to or not he would intervene and seek revenge on my behalf; I could always be sure that the offender would not bother me again - well in most cases anyway! I didn't necessarily always condone his behaviour, but his brotherly protection did make me feel safe, secure and loved. I truly adored him. He did so much to help me over the years with his protection and brotherly support. He didn't really help me with my schoolwork; that wasn't his 'bag'. He was never interested in education. However, he taught me to ride my first two-wheel bike and I remember it as clearly as if it were yesterday, partly because it was the first big present that I had ever had and also because it was brand new to me (as most things were passed down the line). This was just mine and I was simply thrilled with it. It was a blue and red Raleigh, vibrant colours and chrome gleaming. It was my pride and joy. I can still smell the oil on the chain. I simply couldn't believe my eyes when I was told to go behind the sofa on Christmas morning and there it was under a sheet. I shrieked with delight.

The last and dearest of my siblings is my wonderful sister, Diane, who is five years older than I am. Her love and support has always been there right from when we were young and living at home through to the present day. She helped me with and taught me about so many things, sometimes through her own mistakes and experiences, but mainly through being the brightest and cleverest of the family by far. She has always been there for me, whatever and whenever a situation or problem occurred. I have always known I could rely on her one hundred percent.

I cannot deny that we've had our moments, naturally. We certainly did, especially when we were growing up and sharing a room. She hated it if I used her make-up or her Charlie perfume, which was her favourite. After spraying it you could smell it all through the house so I could never hide that I'd used it. Also, I would help myself to her accessories, necklace and earrings, even her clothes as we got older. Sometimes I would even dare to hang my posters on her side of the wall in the bedroom we shared, past the invisible dividing line. Her side of the wall was covered with David Cassidy posters, and mine with David Essex, although we each secretly had crushes on them both.

Diane was the one that helped most with my school work, painstakingly and constantly teaching and testing me on all the times tables, how to tell the time, how to write an essay, all the way through to preparing for my CSE and GCE exams. She would test me repeatedly, until the night before I sat the papers. She had the patience of a saint and I know I must have been very challenging for her at times. She never gave up until she knew I had well and truly grasped it.

Over recent years, we have become extremely close, partially due to our maturing relationship, but also a result of Diane's sudden and unexpected illness, something for which one can never prepare. Despite this, she has always shared her advice and provided a caring and firm shoulder on which to cry. I cannot thank her enough. She is just the perfect sister and, above all, a most dear, loyal and trusting friend in whom I can confide about anything. I love her immeasurably.

# CHAPTER TWO

Five years after I was born my parents were forced to move; the house we were living in belonged to my grandmother and she wanted to sell it to add to her fortune, or that's what we assumed; she was always preparing for 'a rainy day'! It appeared to me that she never spent a penny on anything but business and hats. She always wore a hat, whatever the occasion and wherever she went. Although her clothes were dated she was always entirely colour-coordinated and smart in her dress.

Nana, as we called her, had built her own little empire running a very profitable and successful baker's shop. She part-owned a smaller grocers as well as owning two small properties, both of which she rented out. One of these properties was the one we all lived in. For Nana, who was primarily the successful businesswoman, nothing else mattered to her but money. She was hard, fearsome, and extremely strict; she used to terrify me. Not once do I remember her sitting me on her lap, or holding my hand, let alone giving me a kiss or a cuddle. Not even so much as a giving me a sweetie; she had a very sweet tooth so sweets were always in plentiful supply, but for her pleasure only. She was completely devoid of any loving or caring emotion towards anyone at all.

Nana had been doing the books in the small office at the rear of the shop one day when she heard someone making enquiries to one of her assistants about accommodation to rent and whether they could put an advertisement in the window. They were prepared to pay as much as two pounds a week in rent – which was almost double what my parents were paying – with a view to hopefully buying a home after six months. Nana's ears pricked up and she went to the front of the store. She always made a point of saying there were to be no favours given to her offspring, nor any favouritism (Mum was the second youngest of seven siblings); letting them live there had only been a temporary measure, but by then they had been there for almost fourteen years. Nana had decided it was time for us to move out. Hard, unloving and heartless, she had no conscience about telling Mum that we had to move.

Nana had lived alone for quite some considerable time as my Grandad had passed away a number of years before I was born, when he was in his late sixties. He was said to have been a most delightful and patient man; indeed, his patience had often been admired. Friends and neighbours used to think he deserved a medal for his tolerance with Nana and in my later years, I could clearly appreciate exactly why.

The search for Mum and Dad to find a place for us all to live began. To be honest, we had outgrown the house, but as properties large enough to house the six of us were few and far between in the town, the task became even more challenging. The weeks rushed closer to the date that we had been given by which he had to vacate the property. The new tenants were coming from another county; the husband was a doctor coming to work at the hospital, which was only a short distance from the house, making it an ideal base for him.

Mum and Dad could not afford to get onto the property ladder to purchase their own house, so they were forced to admit defeat when they were offered a brand-new council dwelling, something they were reluctant to do at the time. The house was on Walney Island, about three miles from the centre of Barrow.

Barrow-in-Furness was where we belonged and was where my parents, grandparents and great grandparents had been born and brought up, generations before my birth. Barrow was historically part of Lancashire but during the 1974 boundary changes it found itself (much to my father's disgust I hasten to add) part of Cumbria. It was nicknamed the 'English Chicago' because of the sudden and rapid growth in its industry, due to economic stature and overall size.

In fact, it was once dubbed by the Telegraph as the "Capital of blue collar Britain" because of its strong working class identity. It was also often jokingly referred to as the longest cul-de-sac in the country, because of its relatively isolated location at the tip of the Furness peninsula. The shelter between Barrow and Walney Island was the ideal location for the shipyard, which grew to provide the core of Barrow's livelihood. The first ship that had been built there was the *Jane Roper*, launched in 1852 and Barrow soon thrived around the yard.

I neither knew nor cared of all this history and the surrounding stories in my early years. My home was Barrow, the only place I had ever known. We didn't have a car and public transport for six of us was not cheap, so my parents could ill afford to venture far.

Nevertheless, the date of our forced move was fast approaching, so in spite of Mum's reluctance we all had to take the twenty-minute bus ride from the town to view the house. We had to travel over two bridges to get to it from the mainland, which for us children, myself in particular, was a most exciting prospect indeed. Walney to me was another world. I couldn't help nor hide my excitement, noticing all the boats and ships bobbing up and down on the channel in varying states of repair. The boats exhibited a wonderful mix of colours, with some clearly rusting badly, rotting and generally looking neglected. Many others gleamed like brand new. I could just make out the names a few of them: *Razzle Dazzle*, *Pure Pleasure* and *Wye Not* were among them, but my favourite of all was *Aye Sea U*, which made me laugh aloud.

Another thing I saw that day which made quite a lasting impression was a huge black hulk, which my father told me was a nuclear submarine. It was towering above the dry dock, where it was busily being worked on by so many men, some of whom I could see atop the high scaffolding. It seemed as if there were hundreds of men, not only working on its exterior but also busy inside it, too, carrying out all kinds of tasks. Dad used to talk about it, but I'd never really understood his chatter until now. Of course, this was what Barrow did – and still does. It's what Barrow is known for. I was amazed.

I also learned that day about some of the various tradesmen: welders, painters, plumbers, electricians, riveters and fitters, to name but a few. Many of these would be tucked away deep inside the bowels of the vessel, under water, doing numerous important jobs. Vickers, the company that owned and ran the yard at the time, employed a workforce of around 12,000, a considerable percentage of Barrow's 72,000 population.

For most of the tradesmen or 'shop floor workers' it was compulsory to wear boiler suits of various colours. The colour was relevant to the individual tradesman, such as blue (the most common one) for a labourer (of which my Dad was one) or white for a foreman. Helmets had to be worn in certain areas around such a potentially dangerous and huge site, these also serving to identify the job they were doing, or the seniority of the role.

This immense vessel looked such a huge beast lying there in the dock; quite an eerie sight. Several years later, I had the tremendous thrill of being invited to go aboard a submarine, which was not only a great honour but also a truly amazing experience. I felt quite emotional to be allowed to stand inside and see the workmanship from top to bottom, front to back, inside and out, or at least the areas permissible or open to us.

My memories of seeing all that was involved in not just the building of this first Trident submarine but imagining the future and history that would follow left me with a feeling of unforgettable pride. Seeing how and where the crew had to live and work on board, sleeping in tiny bunks with hardly any room to breathe or turn over in bed was quite unforgettable.

Then there was the crammed galley where they had to all sit hunched together to eat, in maybe two or three sittings. I had seen several of these vessels being built over the years, either in dry dock or submerged with just the conning tower in view, and I realise had rather taken them for granted until the visit.

The different creaks and groans were haunting. I stood still for a moment and closed my eyes then imagined the feeling of being on board when that hatch slammed shut in readiness for their journey to wherever and whenever they were called. It made me feel instantly claustrophobic but I am sure the crew were used to it. Even so the first time must have been quite trying even for them. We could never know where it was going or where it had been on its covert missions.

The visit gave me a great sense of pride in the shipbuilders and the crew who would sail on the many missions. It was such a wonderful insight and an honour; this truly was a most powerful lasting memory and one I shall take proudly to my grave.

On our approach to the second bridge all the traffic had stopped and an alarm was sounding. I could see two little red lights flashing as the two halves of the bridge rose and opened in the middle to allow the waiting boats to pass. There were two tugboats, preceded by a sailing yacht. I distinctly remember a very attractive lady standing on the deck, wearing white trousers and a red and white striped top. She was also wearing a white cap, peak to the side, with her long blonde hair flowing in the breeze. She was drinking from a tall slender glass, talking and smiling to a handsome younger man who was at the helm. He gently touched her arm, refilled her glass, returned her smile with a proud grin, and winked cheekily at her. I could feel something very special between them even then. I imagined that he was her husband from the way they behaved together.

I was running from one side of the bus to the other, watching it all and trying hard not to miss a thing. I had never seen anything like this before, as we had never had cause or reason to go to the island before. It was all so exciting.

We arrived at our final stop and got off the bus. We all gathered round together and were given strict orders to be on our very best behaviour while Mum inspected our hands and faces. To help pacify us we were each given a treat. I had scented hearts, Diane had crisps and the boys had a chocolate bar each.

We were meeting a man by the name of Martin, who was to show us around the new house to see if we all liked it and we must not let Mum down with bad behaviour or by looking untidy, perish the thought! We knew we would be punished for failing on either account, with all treats to be withheld for one week, early bedtime, or the worst case would be a good smacking (not a pleasant experience I can assure you).

We approached the front door and as soon as it was open, I ran inside and straight up the stairs and into what was the middle bedroom and sat on the wooden floor, quietly waiting. Why that room I am not quite sure but soon I'd fallen asleep after finishing my sweets.

Then, as now, I can fall asleep at the drop of a hat (I apparently once fell asleep in a large cardboard box in our backyard whilst mum had most of the neighbourhood searching for me until Diane found me). On this occasion, Dad came up after a short while to look for me, only to find me asleep curled up next to the airing cupboard with my little rag doll, Melanie, in my arms. I loved that doll. She came everywhere with me. She wore a brightly coloured gingham dress and had a mop of woolly brown hair down to her waist with a yellow ribbon on top. Her big blue eyes were hand sewn in silk with a lovely smile stitched with a fine, dark pink thread.

Dad bent down to kiss my hair, leaving me to sleep and went back down to finish viewing the large lounge, kitchen and scullery room with Mum. There were three large bedrooms, an inside toilet and a separate bathroom. Outside was a very large back garden on an incline that was all laid to lawn, apart from a little soil border crying out for some colour down each side.

My eldest brother, George, then woke me up. He'd crept into the room I was in and jumped on my long blonde curly hair that was trailing on the floor behind me (my Dad would call me Shirley Temple because of it). He then stepped back and trampled on my hand. I let out a scream and began to cry, at which point Mum came charging upstairs, rushed into the room and *I* got a dressing down for being noisy whilst they were talking to the man. George by now had rapidly disappeared into one of the other bedrooms for fear of getting a clip round the ear. Mum then briskly picked me up and took me into the bathroom to wipe my face and clean my hands with a tissue from her handbag (she always had an endless supply of them), but did not notice the large splinters in the back of my hand. She then swiftly ushered me downstairs, as she needed to ask more questions. We were on a tight schedule, as there was to be another viewing following ours and because we had to catch the next bus if we didn't want a long wait for the next one.

I went to join the others who were now all in the back garden sitting on the lawn. Diane was making a daisy chain, Phillip was digging up worms with a large rusty nail he had found in the mud and was searching for any kind of creepy crawlies he could get his hands on. George was talking to the lady next door by the fence,

19

which he'd learnt was called Phyllis. She was hanging out her washing and had come over to talk to him. I went to sit down next to Diane and helped her pick the daisies while she made the chain.

I wanted her to make it as big as possible so we could double it round and give it as a necklace to Mum as a surprise. She said I could give it to Mum when they had finished looking around the house. I was delighted and so excited about giving it to her, as it was very pretty. I held onto it very gently, as it was terribly fragile, whilst looking at it, thinking how clever Diane was to have made it. I then just laid it on my lap while sitting down in the brief burst of sunshine that had appeared. I could see Mum and Dad through the window now when Phillip shouted out that we needed to go back inside.

I rested the chain on the grass whilst I stood up and then bent down to pick it up again. Out of nowhere, George appeared, snatched at it then trampled it to the ground. I once again began to cry, but Phillip had seen everything, ran towards him and pushed him over. He was about to punch him when there was a knock on the kitchen window: it was Dad, so Phillip hesitated and walked away. By now, he had grass stains on the knees of his jeans but he didn't care. He came over, picked me up and took me inside, saying not a word. I could see George smiling triumphantly to himself by the fence thinking he had got away with it this time. I remember hoping that Phillip would remember to sort it later; he wasn't one to let anyone get the better of him, certainly not George.

We all left the house, each of us in different states of mind; I remember feeling very excited about the prospect of living in a lovely big new house with a garden front and back, and bus rides over two bridges to get into town, as did Diane I believe. I don't honestly think Phillip would have minded where he lived; anywhere from here to Timbuktu would be fine by him. George made it perfectly plain that he certainly didn't want to live there, moaning and glaring, his facial expression completely changed. It was unnerving; a look I came to know very well in my later years.

He went on complaining for some time, saying that all his 'mates' (what few he had) lived in the town. The main big park in Barrow was just off Abbey Road, five minutes away from our current house, and he would often disappear there, maybe to go on the paddleboats, something we all did from time to time if we went together on the lake. I never really knew where he went or who he was with, and neither did I care, but there was where he wanted to stay. We just hoped Mum and Dad liked the house enough not to listen to George, as he could often be quite influential to Mum in particular. I used to wonder if it was because he was the "first born." Whatever it was, he always seemed to have some kind of power over her.

We went back home on the bus, the return journey equally as entertaining and thrilling as the outward leg: there seemed even more boats now as the tide was higher, and you could see more people on board, coming home after a day sailing or maybe even longer journeys. Mum and Dad chatted all the way back home and both seemed very happy and relaxed. We reached our stop, all got off and went up the street and into the house. We all did what was requested of us, putting away our best clothes, the dirty washing in the basket (of which there was quite a lot after the grass and mud stains, not to mention sticky sweet finger marks). We tidied our rooms in preparation for bedtime while Mum busily made the evening meal and Dad read some documents given to him by Martin.

That night's meal was sausage with onions, mash and vegetables. We ate well but by today's standards at least, quite plain food. Notwithstanding that, Mum was a great cook, no matter what she prepared, and this meal was one of my favourites, so long as my sausages were well done, almost burnt. We all sat to the table to eat together, as we always did. She was a great believer in us all sitting down to the main meal as a family; she felt it was an important time for talking and simply 'being together'. Only after dinner were we all allowed to have a little time to do our own thing, before either washing or bathing – according the availability of hot water – finally brushing our teeth and heading off to bed.

For me there was usually a story before going to sleep, read to me by either Dad or Diane. That night Diane offered to do it, but before she started reading, she saw my hand was very sore as I had passed her the book. I asked her not to tell Mum as she may shout at me again, and I didn't want any repercussions from George. So she went into Mum's room next door, got the tweezers from her make-up bag and sympathetically, gently, but painfully removed three splinters before washing my hand in the bathroom sink.

I climbed back into bed for her to begin reading. I had chosen *Hansel & Gretel*. I always enjoyed that story, although that time the last words I remember her reading were "The tiny white pebbles gleamed in the moonlight…" before I drifted off to sleep, the end of a very busy day.

# CHAPTER THREE

Four weeks later a big blue van arrived at the front door to take all our belongings, and move us to the Island. I had heard Mum say she would rather not move on a Friday as it was deemed to be 'bad luck', but it was the only day that Door to Door, the removal company, could accommodate us so we had no choice.

Mum and Dad had apparently decided that they would accept the house the night we had all visited (so no heed had been paid to George's outburst). They thought it would be an ideal family home: it was brand new, therefore no maintenance would be required; it had gardens front and back for us to play in safely; more importantly they felt it would be their own. All ties had been severed with Nana, no more feeling beholden to her; that was undoubtedly for them the biggest advantage.

It was all happening with everyone busily doing their bit; fetching and carrying furniture, boxes, bicycles, toys; anything and everything was loaded or forced into the van. One final check around the house and Dad closed the old paint-scuffed red front door for the last time. He stepped back into the road, looked upstairs to double check that he had closed the windows and then posted the key back through the letterbox for Nana to pick up tomorrow when she came to check it over, as she would undoubtedly do, and meticulously so, he knew.

Mum had always been quite house-proud, not obsessive, and given that there were four youngsters in the home she did a wonderful job. Maybe it was partly down to the fact that it wasn't her house and that she was rather in fear of her mother for some reason. Nana didn't visit very often, but Mum felt that she ought to be prepared and keep it "just so" in case of an unannounced visit.

Dad climbed into the van and sat me on his knee in the front. We all waved goodbye to our neighbours. Emily, a retired nurse from next door who had been present at my birth and partly responsible for my delivery, was stood crying, although she was trying hard not to show it. It explained why earlier she had suddenly disappeared when helping us move the last box of my toys from my room into the van. My doll, Melanie, hadn't been packed, of course, and she was in the front with me, safely tucked under my arm. The noisy engine started and, struggling a little with its load, the van slowly pulled away from the house as we set off to our new home and new life.

My Father seemed both sad and excited at the prospect. He was a lovely man, just shy of six foot and rather handsome, if I may say so. He had a marvellous head of thick dark hair. Mum often used to tell him off, as he would plaster it with Brylcreem; she would frequently ask him not to put it on as it apparently made a terrible mess of the pillowcases, which she then had a terrible job to get. Every one of his generation wore it. She would sometimes hide it from him, but he got wise to that and had a spare tub which he kept in his middle drawer. I can smell it now just by thinking of it.

He also never left the house ever without wearing a tie; he had quite a collection that would be laid out neatly in his top drawer so he could put his hand straight on the one he wanted. He really was quite a smart and proud man.

His was lean yet solidly built. In earlier years, he had played rugby for the local team and rugby was undoubtedly his sporting passion. I can see him now sitting on the edge of his seat, glued to the TV, watching it, shouting for his team. He also enjoyed watching cricket and football, but above all, he was rugby man and an avid supporter of Warrington Wolves. He would have loved to have gone to watch them, but his meagre pay would not stretch to that.

There was one other thing about him that people often commented on and that was his year-round suntan. He only had to look at the sun, or even say the word and he seemed to bronze. His friends and colleagues called him "The Italian Stallion"! He was tall, dark and very handsome for sure. Mum always felt very proud to be seen out with him and often said she was lucky to be married to him. I am told that she had been the envy of many of her friends when they started courting. If Mum or any of her friends saw him in the town on a Saturday afternoon, she used to say their hearts would skip a beat. Mum had secretly liked him for some time, I understand, but for some strange reason thought he was out of her league, even though she was a very attractive woman. One day that all changed, I am very pleased to say, when he asked her out.

# CHAPTER FOUR

It seemed to take forever to empty the van and put everything into the respective rooms and bedrooms, as Mum had labelled all the boxes, cartons and bags as a direction to its rightful place on arrival to save some time. She was always so organised about everything; she needed to be with a family our size to look after.

Within a few days, we were almost ship shape, although furniture was rather sparse as this house was indeed much bigger. We had all been allocated our rooms and I was to share with Diane in the smaller bedroom and George and Phillip shared the middle one; there's had to be bigger as they were older. I could never see the fairness of that but that's how it was. If any of us became ill, with chickenpox or anything similarly contagious, Mum used to make us all sleep 'top-n-tail' in the double bed so we would all get it together and get it over and done with.

Mum and Dad naturally had that biggest room and, compared to the one they'd had in the previous house, it was huge. It was such a lovely room, with big double aspect windows making it so bright and airy. The 'Sunshine Room' they called it, for that was often how it seemed to be, simply bursting with sunlight.

Our room was very pretty, at least when it was all finished it was. Mum had bought us both matching lilac candlewick eiderdown covers to sit over the top of the blankets on our bunk beds, and pretty curtains with a floral pattern of the same colour. Mum had even put a little vase of pink and lilac freesias on the windowsill, her all-time favourites, to add a fragrant smell to the room. The boys' room was just a basic boring blue, nothing to get excited about there. I was sure it wouldn't be long before it was a tip, and stinking of George's feet.

Mum and Dad's room would have to wait for new bedding until they could afford to buy it and she wanted a new bed first. She had used all her spare cash that she had saved to make our rooms cosy and homely, and there were much more important things required before hers and Dad's was even looked at she said.

The house proved to be quite costly to run. It was so much bigger than where we used to live, coal was expensive, and the price per bag had just risen that week. Then there were the fifty pence pieces needed feed the electric meter that seemed endlessly hungry, as were four children to feed, especially two fast-growing boys Mum never seemed able to fill as they were forever asking for food. Her grocery bill had grown tremendously in the weeks since living here; maybe there is some truth in the saying that "sea air makes you hungry" as the beach was just at the top-end of the street.

There was added furniture that was needed: a dining table was near the top of her list as the one we'd been using in the old house was Nana's and she wouldn't let Mum have it, as it had been passed to her from her mother and lent to us as a purely temporary measure. The fact that we'd had it for years meant nothing to her. She didn't need it, she used to check it every visit for scratches, making sure Mum always had a thick cover

over it. The cover was a green army rug she used and a white starched tablecloth on top. Nana was such a hard and difficult woman.

We were now reduced to using an old pasting table for the time being. Dad had made a central support to stop it from dipping in the middle and make it a little more secure. Mum always put the tablecloth on it to try at least make it look a bit nicer, sometimes even a few flowers from the garden, not that we had many – there were more important and pressing things to do before that was tackled. However, she would always put a few in the middle: daffodils, tulips or sometimes the odd rose or two.

She would often say, "One day we shall have a proper mahogany dining table with six matching chairs, I promise, and a big glass vase brimming with flowers handpicked from our own garden." She would sometimes smile and go on to say that "Our first meal together on our new table will be a full Christmas dinner, whenever I manage to buy it, even if it's summertime!" She did make the best Christmas meal you ever could eat, but I do remember wondering whether it would taste the same in the summertime? Can you even buy turkeys that time of year? One thing I did know for sure was that she meant what she said.

One afternoon sometime later, I heard Mum talking quietly to Dad whilst I was asleep on the sofa, or so they thought. She said that she was going to have to find a job to help with things. Dad had been doing lots of overtime in the shipyard where he worked to earn extra cash, but he was tired and it was becoming more noticeable to us all. Generally, he was very placid, but these last few weeks he had become rather irritable and short-tempered and the effects were sadly reverberating through the house. When he was at home he was mostly sleeping (Mum used to say I think he could fall asleep on a clothesline) and the effects of these long days were beginning to show on him as he wasn't getting home until after seven in the evening.

He wasn't very happy at the idea of her going out to work. He felt it undermined his role as breadwinner: it was his duty to take care and provide for his wife and family; he was the man of the house after all, the king of his castle. He also thought Mum had enough to do looking after the house and us all. However, he did eventually have to agree with her, as much as it pained him to do so. He admitted that they were struggling and that any extra cash would be a great help. He'd also been worrying about their situation, unbeknown to Mum, and he was tired (the ten-year age gap at times did present itself). He admitted to her that he was aware that they needed more money coming in.

I pretended to wake up after my usual afternoon nap. I think they had almost forgotten I had been there as I gave Mum a bit of a start when I moved and pushed Dad's jumper off my legs where he'd placed it to keep me warm. Mum turned to Dad and for him not to say anything to us, not to let on that anything was wrong.

Mum was the brains of the pair. She was always the one to sort out the money, the "housekeeping" as she called it, on top of all the other things she managed. She was level-headed, confident and a genius with figures. She had a great personality and was very fit as her passion was dancing, especially Ballroom. She and three girlfriends went on to dance semi-professionally, but it all had to stop once Phillip came along. Emily helped look after George from time to time, but Mum thought that to ask or expect her to look after two boys was just far too much. She did manage to do the odd night here and there but it was quite rare.

Mum kept herself trim and watched what she ate most of the time, partial to the occasional piece of Bourneville chocolate. She was a very attractive woman even in her maturing years, with her naturally curly shoulder-length blonde hair. She always took her time to put waves in her hair with her fingers whilst still damp. She also took care of her appearance and was envied by many, both men and women. I often I saw men turn to give her a second glance as she passed them by in the street, although she I know was completely oblivious to such attention. I remember one man was so busy watching her that he walked head first into a lamp post and at pains to hide his embarrassment ran into the nearest shop to hide. It did make me laugh. I was always very proud of my immaculate Mum.

One thing I can certainly say was she was a real hard worker. I used to hear her until late most evenings, sometimes into the early hours, pottering around doing her jobs quietly while the rest of the house was sleeping. When we were at home, she liked to spend time with us, not doing housework. She was a caring parent, but not a particularly demonstrative person. I always felt she was a little 'uncomfortable' when it came to displays of love and affection; maybe that was a result of her own harsh upbringing and of course, she couldn't be blamed for that.

By contrast Dad was very demonstrative and affectionate, quite exceptionally so. He loved his kisses and cuddles as much and as often as he could get them and that never changed for as long as I can remember. So perhaps, to me anyway he more than made up for the both of them.

Following on from the conversation I'd overheard, I don't think Mum really wanted to go to work as, like Dad, she felt it an admission of defeat or, to a degree, maybe a sense of failure on her part. They had little option really, other than to move to a smaller property on the island, but they didn't really want to move us all again, not now Diane and I had settled beautifully into our new schools, as our latest school reports had recently confirmed. Both schools were but a stone's throw from the house and therefore very convenient: mine was at one end of the drive, with the sea and beach only a couple of hundred yards away at the other end; Diane's school was no more than a short easy walk for her. Everything about living there was so right and as Mum would say, "If it's meant to be it will be."

Both the boys stayed on at the school in town where they had been since toddlers. They now travelled on the school bus each day, and as they were older, our parents had decided it was not a feasible option to move them at that time, so just let them finish their schooling where they were.

# CHAPTER FIVE

"I will strike whilst the iron is hot," Mum said, and the very next day after she'd spoken honestly to Dad about their finances. She felt their conversation had gone more positively than she had anticipated so bought the local Evening Mail paper and scoured the job pages to see what she could find to suit not only her, but equally importantly it had to fit in with us, as she wanted for it to cause as little disruption at home as was possible.

Just as she was pouring over the pages noticing there was just nothing suitable for her at all, she turned the penultimate page and stumbled over an ad for an usherette, mainly evening work. A little unsure about its description or just what the vacancy entailed, she decided to try it. She applied in writing that very evening, after sending Diane and I to the corner shop to buy a nice plain white writing pad with matching envelopes, saying she wanted to write to my aunt in Leeds. This may have been true as they did write from time to time, as we didn't have a telephone at home then.

After completing the letter, she checked it through thoroughly and took it to the post box so it would be collected at first post the following morning. The closing date was not for another week, and although she never expected to hear anything back, she hoped an early submission would give her a better chance. Lo and behold, she was taken completely by surprise to receive an invitation just two days later for an interview to be held at two o'clock the next day. She was quietly pleased. Mum was never one to outwardly display any great sense of excitement or feeling, but we all got to learn her little quirks of course, and know what her different tone or facial expressions really meant.

She attended promptly, in fact, she caught the earlier bus in case the bridge went up as that would make her terribly late, and that wouldn't possibly do, as it was to her "very rude and discourteous to be late." That was something she drummed into us, as we got older. Looking very smart in a two-piece dogtooth checked suit and coral blouse, with stiletto-heeled shoes and matching bag, she entered the office promptly and shook hands with a confidence, which surprised even her. It all happened so quickly that she hadn't really had the time to think about nerves or any serious preparation. Though Mum was a very confident woman anyway and nerves were something she never appeared to suffer, she hadn't worked for so long and her last job was only at a dry cleaner's where she had worked for a number of years until just before having George at nineteen years old. However, she also was a big believer in fate and a fond user of the phrase, "If it's meant to be it will be."

The job really was simply seeing people to their seats when they entered the cinema; she would be armed with a big bright torch to use to help people that arrived late when the lights had gone down to see them to their seats. Even into the start of the film some people would arrive, something she always thought bizarre, as they have missed the gist of the film. Then during the intervals, she carried a huge heavy tray laden with ice cream tubs and blocks of all flavours, drinks, popcorn and so much more. I never knew how she ever managed to carry it all. I used to watch her fill her tray from the enormous freezers in the cold room and sometimes I would be allowed to help. She would then put a thick leather strap over her shoulder and round her neck and slide the tray towards and check the light on top was working before lifting it down.

I often thought she would topple over, as it seemed so heavy and full. She was such a very slender woman though she did have a rather generous bust. Off she would then go and make her way to her allocated space to be in place for when the lights went up at the edge of the stage. Then, as the lights would go up as the interval began, she would instantly be mobbed by a hoard of hungry or thirsty viewers. She always added up the prices of everything in her head. I never could understand how she managed to do it so quickly and precisely.

Soon the lights would very slowly dim again, a sign that the interval was over and the film was to resume, urging people to head back to their seats promptly and ensure they were sat quietly in time for the film to commence. Mum would then head back to the foyer, usually with an empty tray. Night after night she did this and must have taken a small fortune over the three or four days she worked each week.

Things at home got back to normal because of her extra income. In fact, they were even better as they managed to buy a few new bits of furniture, well, new to us anyway from the saleroom in town. The first thing was the dining table and then came the chairs. Mum did have an eye for furnishings as well as a good bargain. As promised and true to her word the day the chairs arrived we did indeed sit down to a Christmas dinner. It was August, but a promise was a promise.

After that, every Sunday without fail we would sit down to a roast dinner with all the trimmings followed by her home-made rice pudding, tapioca or semolina. Then we would sometimes be given a choice of meals in the week, rather than sitting down to eat what was put in front of us. She always bought her meat fresh every day from the butchers up on the corner of the drive. So, at breakfast she would ask "Would you all like shepherd's pie? Or Lancashire hot pot? Or maybe sausage and mash tonight?" We all had to have the same, but it was nice to have some choice. That said, we rarely agreed, and as she would never cook different things for any of us she would often decide. Whatever the meal, we always ate together at the same time – that was her rule.

We had treats from time to time, too, nothing too much as money was tight, so often it would be a comic or magazine. *Twinkle* for me, *Jackie* for Diane and *The Dandy* and *The Beano* for Phillip and George as they never grew out of reading them. Sometimes it might even be a book, or occasionally for me it may be a new dress or top. If I were very lucky, I would get my favourite thing of all, a pair of shoes. I have always loved new shoes; to this very day they are my true weakness. I can put on a new pair of shoes and they instantly make me feel different somehow, a bit like I imagined Judy Garland in the film *The Wizard of Oz* must have felt when put on the sparkly red slippers, then clicked her heels together to take her home.

That film was, I hasten to add, one that I grew to absolutely loathe, as I had to watch it every single day

37

for two weeks on its release, sometimes even twice a day, as I had to go into work with Mum as I couldn't be left alone. I was given a bag of popcorn or a packet of Payne's Poppets, both of which today are still firm favourites of mine. She would always sit me near the back so she could check on me frequently. I knew that film all off by heart almost word for word and back again by the end of the first week. More importantly, I knew when to hide my face when the Wicked Witch of the North appeared! I was terrified of her. I will always remember the relief I felt during the last scene after she had had water thrown at her, rubbing her hands, shrieking "I'm melting, melting!" until she disappeared under her cloak and hat. Almost as scary for me were the Munchkins or Oompa Loompas; I used to shut my eyes tight and put my fingers in my ears and hum quietly to myself, counting the seconds when I knew they had left the screen. However, although I loathed that film, it was still far better than being left at home with George.

Mum really seemed to enjoy her job and of course, the extras it allowed her to buy, for her an added bonus, almost like a personal sense of independence or achievement. In turn, this seemed to make her much happier, too. She felt she was contributing to the home. Dad wasn't as tired as he didn't have to work quite so much overtime, and the house was beginning to look more like a home, our home.

At work she had started to take on additional tasks from time to time, sometimes due to staff sickness. Things like operating and managing the kiosk, working in the ticket office, ordering stock, or balancing the stock books (as she was such a whiz with figures). Or filing paperwork for Harry, her boss, in his old dark dingy office, and answering his phone on occasion if he was busy with a rep or staff member or overseeing some technical problem. It all seemed to add variety to the job to the point where she suddenly realised that she was beginning to love it.

One day, completely unexpectedly, she went into the office after doing a stock-take in the kiosk, she put the ledger back on his desk and Harry her boss asked her for a quiet word.

"Sit down a moment I have something to ask you." She sat somewhat pensively and waited. "I would like you to consider an alternative role here. I don't want you to answer me now but I would like an answer by the end of tomorrow. He told her what would be expected of her in this new role, and left her to ponder. Completely shocked at this unexpected offer, she was at the time unsure of what to do about it; she was totally unprepared for it as he had never even hinted anything to her before. "Do you want to be my Assistant Manager?" The words rang in her ears.

They had always got on very well, both at work and as friends. All four of them: Harry and his wife, mum and dad. Together they would socialise from time to time, usually consisting in a night of playing cards, taking it in turn at each other's' houses. They would play for matches mostly, occasionally gambling pennies. She had found an old large Bells whisky bottle out walking one day and she would drop her winning pennies into it from her purse at the end of each day on her way to bed. Occasionally she would take twenty or thirty pence out for her and Dad to have a bet; any winnings all had to go immediately back into the bottle at the end – this was a proviso to which she stuck rigidly. Once the bottle was half-full, about £10, she would then change it into notes and save it in one of her pots up on the top shelf of the kitchen cupboards.

The more she thought about the offer of this new role, the prospect of what the job entailed and the implications to her daily routine, the more it started to sink in. Nevertheless, Harry would be there and he had been a very good friend as well as her boss; she thought he would help if there was a problem and anyway surely he wouldn't have suggested it to her if he didn't think her capable. He had become very fond of the whole family by now and we all became attached to "Uncle Harry" as we were told to address him.

She went home and talked it over with Dad as this was a very big decision, not only because of the increased responsibility, but because of the additional commitment it would entail, as she would of course have to be there in Harry's absence when he was on leave or on his day off. After much deliberation she decided maybe her years of being an usherette was over, lifting that heavy ice cream tray night after night, and that the challenge was one worth taking. So she agreed to do it on a trial basis for a couple of months if he would allow it. "Of course," he said and she proudly became the Assistant Manageress one month later, and with a handsome pay rise included.

Harry had arranged for some alterations to the huge vacant space upstairs that had previously been used for storing old equipment, posters, stands and old film reels, some of which were truly years old some must even have been antique. In truth, it had become a dumping ground over the years. However, the space was to become an open plan office, converted for them both to share. He hadn't told her of this, as he didn't want to pressure her, even though he had arranged for the building work to commence in just two days' time. He wanted her to make the decision on her own and not to be influenced by anything or anyone at all and that was exactly what she did.

# CHAPTER SIX

One month later, she began her new managerial role. All the alterations converting the previously unused junk space were now complete and what a transformation it was. They were both very pleased with the result. In fact, it had turned out far better than Harry had hoped; he wasn't into these kinds of things at all. Had it been just him, it would have stayed as it was. The first important thing for her to get her teeth into was the office layout, something she had been very keen to be a part of from the start, as she wanted to ensure that it was all well laid out and a welcoming and comfortable area in which to work.

The office was on the corner of the building on the second floor and therefore had the advantage of huge windows from floor to ceiling that wrapped around the corner of the building. The room had an almost Rennie Macintosh feel about it and the potential was limitless. She loved this space and saw it as part of a great personal challenge to complete the transformation to absolute perfection.

Her new oak desk had just arrived, all wrapped and protected with huge sheets of cardboard and cellophane bubble wrap. It was to be put correctly into place by the two men awaiting her instruction; she knew exactly where it was to be placed. Harry had kept his old table as he felt an attachment to it over the years; he said it had 'character' and it was to be placed next to hers, at a slight angle, so that he would be the first person anyone entering would see – he was the boss after all.

Then in came the filing cabinets for all the hordes of paperwork required to be stored accurately in date sequence and order of importance. New stationery was to be stored in the storeroom, where it would be locked away and distributed as and when required by Mum, as an attempt to monitor wastage. Then there were lockable files for all important and private documents such as personal staff information, including salaries, addresses, etc. These were to be placed securely next to the safe behind the doors and out of view.

The telephones were to be placed to the right of each desk and she had even thought of simple things such as coloured pens for marking-up documents and a coat stand. There was to be no more dumping damp coats over the back of his winged chair as she thought as it looked untidy and unprofessional. She had even ordered a frame for one of the old posters that once hung in the foyer for advertising one of her favourite films, *Doctor Zhivago*! This was to be hung on the wall directly in front of her desk, she mused to herself, to the left of the lovely big window, so the sunshine didn't bleach it and so that Omar Sharif could watch her busily working. He was one of her all-time heroes and he always made her smile.

Mum had also chosen a lovely ruby red carpet to be fitted under their desk area, as the stripped floorboards were in beautiful condition and a dreadful shame to be hidden from view completely. The window cleaners had arrived on time and were busy outside, quite a task as she was unsure when they had ever been done. After cleaning the outside of the windows they were to come up and do all the insides first thing the next day, ahead of the new drapes that were to be delivered and hung.

It was all looking exactly as she wanted and naturally had gone perfectly to plan. She was delighted with it all. Harry had been watching her enthusiasm and pleasure at seeing it all take shape. This was going to be a very nice place to work and he knew she was the right person for the job. Tomorrow was to be down to business and he would see how she coped with the job in hand, but for now, he was very happy she had accepted the role and although she didn't then know it, the area manager was visiting to see how the alterations had gone and to wish her well with her promotion.

The next morning Mum arrived just after 9 a.m., having caught the earlier bus, to see that the window cleaners were waiting in the doorway for her, having paid heed to her insistence and assertiveness about being prompt. They began immediately inside and the room suddenly looked so light and airy once the windows were rid of the years of accumulated dust, dirt and the husky remains of every kind of insect imaginable. It was incredible. She was almost sorry to have to hide the lovely paned windows with drapes, but she had bought some huge chrome fleur-de-lys-shaped hooks that she had seen in the shop when she ordered the curtain fabric. These were to be fixed to the wall to use as tiebacks if necessary.

The windows were just too much of a feature to be completely ignored and covered up all the time; they were the icing on the cake she thought. The three pairs of heavy lined red and silver curtains were hung and they looked simply stunning. Soon afterwards, the poster had been put up in its silver frame directly in front of her desk where she had precisely pen-marked its position. Once again it brought a smile to her face when she looked at it.

It was almost noon and her personal challenge was now almost complete. All that was left was for the electrician to hang her one piece of "extravagance." It was not extravagant because of its cost, but it was a rather lavish piece, being a large, but delicate chandelier that she had acquired from the antique sale down the street. She had made a cheeky offer for it and asked that they clean it within the price. They of course obliged; not many people said no to my Mum very often and not if they knew what was best for them; behind her confident and attractive persona she could give the best of folk a run for their money, putting them in their place often with just a mere glance. A trait I do believe I may well have inherited along the way.

At one o'clock, Harry arrived. He had been to a meeting at head office first thing so missed all the flurry of activity. He was amazed when he entered the office, holding a huge bouquet of flowers, which he presented to her as a thank you for all her hard work and for agreeing to accept the job as his 'Assistant Manager'. The area manager soon followed Harry, having been talking to Jimmy the projectionist in the foyer as he arrived. He joined in with congratulations and continued to inspect the alterations.

These of course met with his approval and he continued to compliment her on her exquisite taste in decor. She was pleased and thanked him, shrugging it off nonchalantly. She was never one for fuss and compliments. I don't think she really was ever aware of her full potential. To her this was her job and always did everything to the best of her ability – I that was what she felt she was paid for. I knew she'd loved every minute of this project though.

The next day she began the real work and everything just seemed to be falling into place. Every task Harry gave her she completed without question, problem or query. Nothing ever fazed her; she managed all the paperwork, organised meetings, dealt with various staff problems, holiday requests, balanced all the books, and answered the phone on almost the first ring (mainly because she couldn't bear the constant "*tring-tring*" tone). She was very efficient and professional at all times. It wasn't long before Harry soon began to wonder how he had ever managed without her. The place ran like clockwork and the staff was motivated and helpful. But the main thing he noticed was the increase in ticket sales, it was quite astonishing. Mum believed that this had nothing to do with her but the books looked impressive by the weekend when she had to balance them.

This new job somehow seemed to change her in many ways and mostly for the better I had thought. She was very much happier as she felt fulfilled and much more confident; she was more than simply a mother and housewife now, earning a good salary. She was understandably more tired as she was away from home more, often away in the evenings, sometimes quite late.

I suddenly began to miss her, as she was away extra days, especially the evenings. It was a huge change to how things had been at home, and it inevitably meant we all had to take on a few duties and jobs around the house to help lighten the load for her. Sadly, one of George's jobs was to look after me from time to time.

I had come home from school one afternoon to find Dad leaving the house almost as I arrived. He had learnt at lunchtime that one of his sisters had been admitted to hospital and the doctors were unsure at this stage what exactly was wrong; they thought it was a suspected heart condition but they needed to run further tests to establish the problem, so he was going to visit her.

She lived on her own as she had never married and as the eldest brother, Jack, lived in Leeds, Dad thought it his duty to be there with her that evening. Phillip had a woodwork class at night school and Diane was staying over again at my aunty's with our cousin Jean; they were similar ages and were very close friends. Dad used to laugh and say they had become joined at the hip as they spent so much time together. This all meant that George had been told to stay in to take care of me. It was the first time he had done so and didn't seem to quibble, as he wasn't doing anything anyway. He never did do anything; he seemed to live in his room most of the time. I was never sure what he did in there, but that was where he would usually be.

I was up in my room quietly listening to a new tape in my cassette player when I thought I heard a noise. I switched off the player and listened for a moment but could hear nothing, so turned it back on and lay on my bed trying to listen hard as I wanted to learn all the words by heart. It was the Bay City Rollers singing 'Bye, Bye Baby'. Suddenly I heard another dull thud; the boys' room was next door so I stood outside their door to listen – we were forbidden from entering his room at any time, he always made that perfectly clear. I stood and waited to see if the noise was coming from inside. Everything was silent so I started to head back to my room, then like a bullet, he tore up the stairs two or three steps at a time, reached out grabbed me roughly by the arm and started to shake me, shouting and accusing me of going into his bedroom.

"No I didn't!" I promised him. I explained that I'd heard a terrible noise and had just been listening outside his door to see if it was him and check if he was OK. He glared at me, his eyes wild and flashing, and in a split second he picked me up twisted me around threw my legs over his shoulder and slid me down his body. Grabbing me tightly by the ankles, he then proceeded to suspend me head first over the highest point of the stairs and began swinging me back and forth, stopping just short of smashing my head against the wall.

When, through my tears and between sobs I realised he was laughing the whole time, a most haunting laugh, I started screaming, begging him to stop. Tears were pouring down my face but he just kept on and on, then suddenly he let one leg slip from his grip, finding it even more amusing. Holding on to my right leg now with both hands, this seemed to give him a faster swing somehow, which pleased him even more. I held both hands out to stop my head from smashing into the wall or the light fitting. Suddenly, my left elbow clipped the corner of the wall and, suspended about ten feet in mid-air, I started to wretch.

He instantly stopped when he saw vomit splash the walls and down onto the stair carpet; slowly he raised me up and lifted me over the bannister, laying me down on the landing. He turned me roughly over as I began to scream with pain from my elbow and I was violently sick all over the landing carpet and splashed him. He brought me a glass of water and made me drink it all, then sat with me a moment before fetching from the kitchen a bowl of warm soapy water with a drop of Dettol in it. He laid it by my side and as I stood up to run into my room he pulled me back and said, "You're going nowhere until you clean this entire mess, lady."

"But it was your fault," I dared to say, at which point he grabbed my hair, his face inches from mine, and bellowed, "It's your mess and you will clean it up, every bit of it. *Then* you can go to your room. I don't want to see you and don't you dare tell any of this to anyone. Or else!" At which point he smirked and started to laugh, and gave me a look, "that look", the one I came to recognise only too well. Terrified and with no option I did as I was told whilst he stood and watched over me, grinning to himself the whole time. I was cleaning mostly one handed as my arm was hurting now, but I dared not tell him that, as that would have pleased him more I was sure.

He bent down to pick up the bowl when he was satisfied I had finished and poured the remains down the toilet which was in the room just behind us. I went into my room and I undressed removing the foul-smelling damp clothes I wore. I then heard the front room door slam shut. I went into the bathroom and stared to wash my face and clean my teeth before creeping into my room, closing the door, drawing the curtains and climbing in bed, sobbing. I was shaking with shock and wanted my mum. I lay thinking of all that had just happened: what if he had dropped me, why or how did it all happen? I still felt scared, but was by now feeling very tired.

"Susan! Wake up, you're going to be late for school and you need to have breakfast!" Mum shouted from the kitchen. I lay trying to open my eyes, feeling so tired, when suddenly I remembered having a most horrible dream, and turned over to see the clock and my arm hurt. Sadly, it wasn't a dream and I suddenly remembered it all so well.

I went downstairs and into the kitchen. Dad and the boys had gone by now. I reached up into the cupboard to get a bowl for my cereal and I winced; Mum noticed and asked me what was wrong. I said it was nothing. Starting to feel a little nauseous again, I sat down, no longer feeling hungry. I said I didn't have time to eat anything, but to Mum breakfast was the most important meal of the day. I just couldn't face it, so I just had a sip of tea that she had poured for me and went back upstairs to get dressed. I came back down ten minutes later all ready to go and she passed me a slice of toast with mixed fruit jam, wrapped in a paper towel to eat on the way. I thanked Mum, left for school and as soon as I was out of sight, I slipped it down the nearest drain.

I arrived at school feeling very odd. I couldn't concentrate on my lessons, not even biology and I loved biology. Thoughts of the night before drifted into my mind and I could feel myself welling up. The teacher came over during break to ask if I was OK. "Yes, of course, Miss, thank you!" I lied. By the end of the day I was feeling very weary. I just wanted to go home and get into bed. George was out that evening so I knew I didn't have to face him; he was going up to Brian's, one of his few friends, to watch a movie. He was in his late teens, so there were no questions asked anymore as to his whereabouts; he just did his own thing more or less, as

50

far as our parents were concerned. He was, I always believed, Mum's blue-eyed boy.

I got home at 4 p.m. and Mum let me in. She had been off that day and it was Thursday, which meant Baking Day. The smell of home baking greeted me as she opened the door. Filling the kitchen was an array of fairy cakes, gingerbread, egg custard tart, jam tarts and currant pasty (or fly pie as Phillip used to call it!). It was all laid out on the kitchen table and spread across the large worktop. I knew it wouldn't last long once the boys were home; they would soon make short work of it. Mum was good at lots of things but being a good cook was at the top of the list. She made me a cup of tea, brought me a piece of gingerbread, and sat down beside me on the sofa.

"You looked a little distracted and distant this morning when you left and seem more tired than usual. You never came down last night to say goodnight and you were fast asleep when Dad and I came in to see you. George said you had been in your room reading all night and even he hadn't seen you. Susan, is everything alright?"

"Yes,", I immediately lied, as I couldn't possibly tell her the truth. "Everything is fine, Mum, just busy at school as we are going to be having exams soon and I hate them, and it means lots of tests and revision. That's all, Mum, don't worry."

My arm was sore and she had noticed me wince as I put my plate on the coffee table. She asked what was wrong with it. "Oh, nothing," I again lied. "I hurt it today playing on the bars in the playground, but it will be fine." She asked to look and I couldn't refuse, so I gingerly lifted my arm and slipped off my jumper, trying

51

to hide the pain, and she saw my elbow. I hadn't looked since last night, mostly because I didn't dare. It was beginning to look very bruised and grazed.

"What a mess!" she exclaimed and began to feel it and gently move to see if it was possibly broken. I started to feel nauseous again, but she satisfied herself that it was only badly bruised, and would check it in the morning and maybe take me to the hospital if she felt it necessary.

I think she had believed my story and that was what mattered to me most now. She sat a little while longer with me then went upstairs to run me a nice bath with her best bubble bath, given to her by Dad at Christmas – she thought it might help bring out the bruising. She brought my best fluffy pink spotty pyjamas and favourite soft lemon towel and put them on the stand in the bathroom ready for when I had finished. She was always caring and kind when I was unwell or hurt. I think she also sometimes felt guilty about working so much but we needed the money so she had to do it.

I climbed into the bath and lay quietly, smelling the light amber aroma of the bubbles, also feeling quite honoured to be given it, as it was quite an expensive present. I know because Diane and I were with Dad when he bought it; we actually chose it for him, a gift set with the perfume and body lotion that you could smell and identify the instant she applied it. It was used only on the odd or special occasion they went out together and that wasn't very often at all.

After I had finished and dried myself as best I could with my injury, I went back down stairs. Mum had bought me a new book that day so I lay on the sofa and began to read it. Within minutes, I was fast asleep. I was woken by the sound of plates and cutlery rattling, and I smelt the tea, corned beef hash, a good northern dish if ever there was one and one of my favourites.

Over the next few days, my arm started to improve and I could once again play on the bars in the playground, something I loved to do. In time, I began to forget what had happened, or at least put to the back of my mind at least. Maybe I had deserved it, I had occasionally thought to myself. Maybe I should just do as he says next time. I shuddered at that thought of him looking after me again.

The new house was a lovely place to live; Mum had it looking beautiful, having now bought all her required bits of furniture and furnishings. She certainly did have nice taste when it came to soft furnishings, as was now evident at home as well as hers (and Harry's) office.

The seaside being so close was an especially great bonus and a novelty that didn't seem to be wearing off. Dad would often take me for a stroll along the beach; we sometimes took a bucket to pick winkles and would take them home to boil them up and eat them. That was a real treat. Mum always hated the smell of the cooking but always enjoyed to join in their consumption.

We sometimes went to the beach to give Mum some uninterrupted time to catch up with her housework as much as anything I think, but also to spend some time together. Mum was rather house-proud by this stage. Things were hard earned and needed caring for. This was now their home and one of which they were really quite proud.

## CHAPTER SEVEN

We had been living on Walney for four years and everything was familiar, almost as if we had never lived anywhere else before. Nana paid the odd visit by bus or sometimes she would hire a taxi. She complained or moaned incessantly from the minute she came through the door until she went back out again. Fortunately, it wasn't very often we saw her. Mum never had much time for her at all, especially since turning us out of our home. However, getting away from her was one of the biggest positives of moving here she often used to say; ultimately, she had done us a huge favour in many ways, but Mum would never admit that to her now of course. I think she was actually rather scared of her, but then I couldn't blame her for that, she really was quite an ogre.

I was in the kitchen washing up after dinner one evening and Mum had just left for work. Dad was going out for his constitutional pint and it took him forever to get ready. It was painful to witness sometimes, but nothing could hurry him, as he was so particular. Today I am sure he would be classed as 'OCD' without any shadow of doubt, far worse than a lot of women (no disrespect to us of course).

So that night I thought Diane could help me with a little revising that I had to do and then we could watch something together on the TV when Dad had gone. I went up to our room to ask her and she was getting changed. I asked if she could help me with my homework and then watch TV together as Dad was going out.

"No, I'm sorry, but I'm going out tonight myself. Diane and I are off to the pictures." Phillip was out with his biker friends so I deduced that George would be staying home. A shudder suddenly passed over me. He had sat with me the previous week and it was fine, so I was just being silly, I convinced myself.

Dad had just left and Diane had come for Diane half an hour ago to get the bus. I went back down to the kitchen and finished cleaning the worktops before I got my homework and put it on the kitchen table ready for later. I put my dirty washing in the bag and went to sit and see what was on the TV for a while as when George came down he would be welded to the chair right in front of it and I wouldn't get to see anything so I started to watch Coronation Street whilst finishing my fairy cake. I thought I would just see the end of it then go into the kitchen to do my homework, leaving him to the TV, staying out of his way before going off to bed. That was the best option, I thought. There was just five minutes left of it when he came in. "I am just watching the end of this then I will go and do my homework and you can sit here. There's only about five minutes left now."

He looked at the clock and said there was actually almost ten minutes left: "Go and put the kettle on quick and you can watch it." I said OK and went into the kitchen; best not upset things. I filled the kettle and put it on the stove. I even got his favourite cup off the drainer ready for him and went back into the lounge where he was now sitting on the chair I had been sitting on. He looked up: "Where is my tea?"

"But you said just to put the kettle on. I put your cup out ready, too."

"Go and make my tea, twerp!" he shouted.

"But I will miss the end—" I started to say before he suddenly he jumped up and slapped me so hard on the bottom that I fell to the floor, landing on my tummy and winding myself. "Please no, not again," I thought, my heart now racing. I began to cry as he came towards me, grabbed one leg and dragged me into the hall. He swiftly opened the door to the under stairs cupboard, picked me up and threw me inside, scraping my shoulder on the door catch on my way in. He then slammed the door and wedged it shut so I couldn't get out. I sat crying. "Why does he do this to me? What is wrong with me?" Was it my fault, as he had said?

I sat and waited. "He will let me out in a minute; it's dark and horrible in here. Surely he won't leave me very long, not this time." So I waited and waited, worrying too as I had to do my homework. I was now beginning to feel very cold I only had a skirt and T-shirt on. I was tired and couldn't breathe properly as it was so small in there. I knocked the door to see if he could hear me, but I was wasting my time. He had turned up the TV.

Suddenly I heard the doorbell ring again and I thought he either hasn't heard or maybe he didn't want to answer it. "Oh please," I was praying, "Please answer it then let me out." Maybe he had forgotten I was in there. Silence fell. I couldn't hear the TV then the lounge door opened, and then the front door. It was Phillip. I heard him say to George as he came in that his friend had dropped him off on his bike, but not to tell Mum, as

56

she wouldn't be pleased at all. Then he stopped talking and asked why the chair was wedged against the door before moving it away.

George obviously hadn't expected Phillip yet and had forgotten to move it. As he went to open the door, I shouted to Phillip who heard me and opened the door. I was shaking; tears streamed down my cheeks. "What on earth are you doing in there?" He of course knew who put me there. He took my hand and helped me up. Looking somewhat confused, he put his arms round me, stroked my hair and waited for me to stop crying. I didn't know what to say for fear of the repercussions, but decided to tell the truth, what George had done; once again I started sobbing but eventually told him exactly what had happened.

Once he was satisfied that I was OK he took me into the kitchen and made me a hot drink. We picked my homework off the table, put it back in my bag and he then carried it upstairs to my room with me in tow. "Now you stay here and do your homework." By now I realised it was after nine o'clock; I had been in there for almost two hours.

"It's too late now and I am tired." I said that I would have to do it in the morning and asked him to wake me early, as it had to be done for first lesson the next day. He said he would and then took my bag back downstairs. I quickly got washed and ready and climbed into bed. Phillip came back up to check I was OK and say goodnight. "Go to sleep and don't come down now will you." I said I wouldn't and settled down with my book.

I heard them talking quietly at first but it gradually got louder and I heard Phillip shout, "If you ever lay a finger on her again it will be the last time, and that's a promise! She is nine years old. What were you thinking? She is terrified up there." The next noise was a loud thump: they had clearly started fighting. They had little punches here and there on occasion and the odd 'play fight' but this sounded much worse. In fact, it sounded quite serious. I put my fingers in my ears to block it out as I was quite scared by now. It didn't go on for too long and I heard the front door slam. I turned over in bed and pretended to be asleep as I thought it was probably Phillip who had gone out and I didn't want George coming into my room to bother me again. Then I heard Phillip on the telephone and I felt safe now, as it was obviously George who had gone out. I drifted off to sleep.

George had by then left school and was working in the shipyard with my dad. He didn't enjoy it, but it was a job. He never seemed to do much from the way he talked. He had one friend, Brian, the brother of Diane's best friend Denise, but otherwise George was quite a loner. He had actually been out on a date recently, his first girlfriend as I recall. He brought her home one evening. Sandra was surprisingly nice, very down to earth and likeable. Even Mum liked her and that was saying something. I thought Sandra must have been out of her mind; what could she possibly see in him? Then maybe she was just what he needed, and so long as she kept him out of my way I was all for it and long may it last.

Well sadly it didn't last: he said he found her too clingy and needy and he didn't like that, so he called it off. There were tears and hysteria and she frequently came to the house crying and begging him back. I couldn't help feel for her, but thinking she was better off out of it, not that I dared say as much, most certainly not, but it meant that he would be home more again and I dreaded that.

As luck had it he found someone else within no time at all, thank goodness, and Anne was brought home and introduced to us all as his fiancée. He clearly hadn't wasted any time there, I thought! She was lovely: quite attractive, nicely dressed and rather posh if I may say. How does he do it? She was clearly far too good for him; that was something he joked about one day, so he knew as much himself. Well Mum was – to say the least – thrilled at the idea of a wedding in the family. He was only nineteen but she was very happy for him.

Sadly, she didn't last either and he again called it off. This one took it even worse than the last and she was constantly phoning the house, trying to catch him going to or coming home from work. She even wrote him letters day after day. All to no avail as he had made his mind up and vanished to Bath for over a month. There was no real explanation; he just seemed to disappear and it was all so sudden, not that it bothered me. On the contrary, I was very pleased about it, of course, for the obvious reason that it meant he wouldn't harass me anymore.

One day when I came home from my friends, Mum and Dad were both at home, as Dad was on his two weeks' leave. Vickers used to close down for 'Shipyard fortnight', as it was then known, when the entire workforce had to take the same two weeks off every year. I was in the kitchen with Mum. It was Thursday and she was in mid-flow of a baking session, although with Phillip now married and George not there, she didn't need to do so much anymore. It was still a lovely spread and the smell – as ever – was delightful and made me feel hungry. I was just tucking in to one of her rock cakes when the doorbell went. I went to answer it as she had her hands in the mixing bowl and Dad was sleeping on his chair in the lounge.

When I opened it there stood George. My heart sank. I remember shaking as he made eye contact with me and stepped into the hall.

"Hi, our kid," he said. "Where are the parents?"

"Dad is sleeping in there so shhh," and I put my finger to my lips. "Mum is in the kitchen baking."

He just pushed me out of the way. I slipped and fell backwards onto the telephone table and caught my back on the corner of it, at which point I heard Mum shout, "Who is it?"

Dad came out of the front room to see me picking up the phone from the floor. He looked up then and saw George. He seemed delighted to see him and they both went into the kitchen, shortly after which I heard Mum begin to cry, clearly equally happy at his return.

I went up into my room and sat on the bed feeling sick, just from the sight of him and the thought that he was now back. He had just walked through the door and it would all start again. I read for a while, cleaned my side of the bedroom, and kept out of the way. I had hoped that Diane and I could have had a room each once George had gone, but no, it was to be kept as it was for when he came back, we were told, almost like a shrine.

Eventually I went back down stairs and I could hear Dad with a slightly raised voice, which was unlike him, especially these days as it was only when the boys had been arguing or fighting did he really shout and as they hadn't been here it was rather unusual. I went into the front room to find Mum sitting on the settee with her head in her hands. She was sobbing, with George sat on the chair in front of her. I looked at George and instantly I realised something was "different" about him: he looked different; his hair was more blonde; he was wearing bright clothes and had a pair of sandals on his feet! OK it was a lovely July day but sandals? Mum asked me to go back upstairs, having assured me that she was fine and not to worry.

I went and I lay on my bed once again and all of a sudden, the light dawned and the penny had dropped. My brother was gay! Suddenly so many things all fell into place, things I had seen or heard in the still of night, hushed phone conversations that seemed odd at the time. There was also his behaviour which, I suddenly realised, was decidedly camp.

Oh dear. That was what they were discussing down there I just knew it was, and I knew my Dad wasn't going to be happy about it at all. My Dad was, if I may use the expression, a 'man's man' and disliked any form of effeminate behaviour; he couldn't watch anything or anyone on TV that even hinted at it in the slightest. It was sadly a taboo subject for him. If you have watched the marvellous film Billy Elliot then my dad was very similar to Billy's father in that respect. This was going to be very interesting, I thought.

I walked into the kitchen, sat at the table, and leant back on the hard, slatted wooden back chair and I felt a bruise from where I had fallen earlier. I kept quiet; I'd had much worse to contend with from him in the past.

Mum put the plated dinner in front of each of us all as Diane was home now, and Dad broke into a bit of a speech. 'Oh I know what's coming,' I thought to myself.

He went on to announce that George was moving out permanently and going to live in London as of the next day! 'Oh thank the Lord,' I said to myself, 'Hoorah!' He refrained from saying why and I wasn't going to force the issue, but the news for me couldn't have been better. Mum was obviously uncomfortable about this and Dad, I could tell, was unhappy to say the least, and I knew for sure it wasn't because he was moving out.

The next day he left at quarter-to-ten to catch the ten o'clock train to London. Mum was in tears as she waved the taxi off and Dad was uneasy as he sat, looking distraught in his chair. We closed the door and went about our duties as though it was a normal day.

# CHAPTER EIGHT

I now attended Walney County Secondary School or "Walney Modern", as it was commonly known. Over one hundred years old, it was a huge and daunting building with blue painted window frames. It had become a joint school with the other secondary school on the island, West Shore. The two schools were arch enemies and always had been since time began, but this joint venture eventually put paid to that and restored a certain form of acquaintance between them. The new school had been gradually extended to house everyone and a few years later the old original school was finally closed, emptied and sadly demolished. It was an unhappy episode for the inhabitants of the Island, with all those years of great education successes stories and so many memories for so many people and their families all crashed to the ground in no time.

West Shore (at the time it pained me to admit) was a very nice school, although the old one was missed by all pupils. It always had an air of superiority because of its history and supposed better class of schooling, this attitude being the cause of its arch enemy status.

This was where, at the tender age of sixteen, I met Paul. He was in my year, but the class above me. I remember noticing him in the school hall talking with a teacher and, at the time, he made no great first impression if I am honest, but I did find myself thinking about him from time to time. Whenever I saw him I would flush embarrassingly and it wasn't until sometime later when I was in the kitchen discussing boys with my closest friend (also called Sue) that I innocently mentioned I liked him. I didn't know his name or anything about him but she knew exactly who I meant.

She was far more worldly than I with her having had a countless number of "relationships", be they one night stands or short term boyfriends lasting literally no more than a week or two in most cases. She was a lovely girl: quite tall, about 5' 6" compared to my 5' 4" (and a bit); she had lovely, darkish hair that had a natural bounce, a very nice figure and (unlike myself) was rather large in the chest department, that being quite an attraction for a large proportion of her male followers. She was a good friend we spent a lot of time together hanging out, sleeping at each other's houses (although she seemed to spend much more time at my house). There was for a long time a part of her that I couldn't quite figure out. I could never quite put my finger on it, but something just wasn't quite right. One day she decided to off load and really open up to me and all became clearer.

Her parents had had a rather messy divorce when she was very young. She had been very close to her father but he had left and moved away so she sadly didn't get to see him very much, and less and less as time went by. She lived with her rather violent mother, who was all too quick and keen to use her fists when the mood took her. At first, I didn't believe her when she told me that her mother used to hit her.

Sadly, on more than one occasion, I was a witness to these beatings. It really traumatised me the first time – I can see it all as clearly as if it were yesterday. I felt hatred and horror that a mother could behave this way and inflict such pain upon her own child. I'd gone through some bullying with George but he never beat me. He slapped me, but never the punching and kicking I witnessed from a mother to her own flesh and blood.

I felt physically sick and so sorry for the poor girl. When I first noticed that she wasn't even crying, not a single tear, I couldn't understand why not. I saw and heard it all, every punch, slap and thump, not to mention a kick in her stomach. It soon sunk in that she wasn't crying because she had sadly become used to it.

Her mother turned then to me once, and I wasn't even sure she was aware of my presence at first as surely she wouldn't have been so "public" about it. She evidently didn't seem to mind at all, explaining, "She deserved that for not doing her chores after school. Now you get yourself off home.

Without further ado, I took my leave and said I would see her in the morning. I only lived a ten-minute walk away from her but I think it was one of the longest walks home; I just couldn't get it out of my head and I started to cry, tears streaming. I felt so sorry for her and was in a state of shock. I went home to an empty house as Mum was at work and Dad was at the cricket club. I turned on the television and pushed on the three various channel selector buttons on the box to find something to take my mind from it.

*Bless This House* was on, which I thought was quite ironic after what I had just witnessed. I sat on the brown velour chair in front of the telly and watched rather distractedly, but I did enjoy it – Sid James and Diana Coupland were a great team. I'd dozed off in the chair and before I knew it, it was quarter-to-ten, with still no sign of anyone coming home. I took myself off to bed.

The next morning I got up after a rather restless night and prepared for school, went downstairs and I told Mum over breakfast at what I'd witnessed. She could not believe it either. We talked about it for a while before a knock at the door announced that Sue had called for me to walk to school with her. I finished my toast and left.

She didn't mention a word about it and I of course didn't want to bring it up – I didn't know how she would react and I didn't want to open wounds or upset her at all. I could see a bruise on her chin and a scratch to her right eye, and it repulsed me. It was 'the proof' that it hadn't been some bad dream. Having seen the marks and bruises, I remembered seeing similar on her before but we never talked about them I just assumed they were from doing sports or gymnastics or something innocent. If only.

I had my domestic science lesson second and third period, which meant a trip on the school bus, as we didn't have kitchens or cookers in the school building. We had to go to old council buildings that had been adapted into a kitchen for such lessons. I made my Apple Charlotte, though with difficulty and a great deal of help from the teacher as I had my arm half in plaster following an operation to straighten my finger after it had been kicked by a boy at the youth club some months before. I packed it away to take home for tea, knowing Dad would be pleased as he always enjoyed a dessert.

We climbed onto the bus and set off back to school. It was only a fifteen-minute ride and we were back just in time for dinner. I loved the school dinners, well most of the time I did. This time the dinner included beetroot, which I disliked immensely. The dinner ladies would walk around the dining room watching everyone eating. One saw that I had left the beetroot on the side of the plate, having polished off the rest of my meal.

Sue and I went to our classroom for the next lesson. She went on ahead as I had dropped my pencil case and stopped to pick it up. When I stood up he was standing next to me (the boy I liked) he gave me a big smile said "Hi," and went back down stairs to his classroom.

Flushed and distracted I walked into my classroom and sat down and I could feel someone looking at me. When I turned around Sue was smiling at me; she didn't say a word, just a huge grin across her face.

The Geography lesson began but I was a little pre-occupied with seeing him so close. The teacher, Mr Redhead, soon brought me out of my reverie by hurling a blackboard rubber across the classroom – something he was known for – which narrowly missed my dressed arm. He asked me a relevant question from his lecture as he was convinced I was not paying attention. I promptly sat forward and I don't know how but I managed to answer it perfectly. Phew, I was saved, thank goodness, as he was a grumpy tyrant. He congratulated me and proceeded pointing at the map in front of him with his stick.

Lesson ended, we went to break and Sue came to tell me that whist I was out this morning she saw Paul and asked him for a date with me. He didn't know who I was, or even my name, so said he would check me out and get back to her. The jigsaw was now starting to make sense, him appearing next to me, her grinning at me. Of course, it all fell into place. She described me as having my arm in a sling so he knew who to look out for. He later got back to her and said that he would definitely have a date with me – that evening!

I had no time to think about it as it had all been arranged and agreed for me at seven o'clock that evening, Wednesday 22nd October 1975, on the seat at the corner of the street near North Walney junior school. I was there and on time but he was almost ten minutes late and I wasn't hanging about feeling stupid, or worse still that I had been stood up. I started on back home when suddenly I heard a voice coming from the field across the road directly opposite. Out of nowhere he was there smiling across at me, before hurrying across the road, apologising for his lateness. He blamed his parents, explaining that as he was leaving the house they began to give him the twelfth degree on the where, who and why was he going out.

I of course accepted his apology and we went for a walk and talked as if we had known each other for years. He made me feel very at ease and I knew he felt the same. It was all just so easy. After that first date, we gradually started to see more and more of each other.

I was in no hurry to meet his family yet, I was far too shy for that. He did mention it from time to time but I just brushed it off with excuses. Until one day he said, "My mum would really like you to come for tea on Sunday." Oh dear. I knew I couldn't refuse again, so I nervously agreed and asked him to thank her for the invitation. It was three days away and I don't think I had ever been so scared.

His father was a policeman, I already knew, and for some reason that was more than a little daunting. I assumed he must be very strict as a result, but time would tell. His mum didn't work; she was a stay-at-home housewife and mother and he always talked very fondly indeed of her. Lastly, there was his only sibling, his brother, John, who was three years older. From what I had deduced, they didn't have the closest of relationships, but then all families are different. I was told they were all going to be there to meet me on Sunday.

As the day arrived, I did start to feel a little easier about it, but also knew I would be glad for it to be over. Paul came to my house for me so we could walk there together, knowing how nervous I was likely to be, and said that they were all looking forward to meeting me. As we got closer to the house the nerves started to kick in once more. I almost wanted to turn back but I couldn't; I had to do it, if only for Paul. He wanted this so much and it was, in all fairness, long overdue.

I was welcomed first by his brother John, as his Mum was out with Penny the dog. I immediately decided that I liked him; he made me feel very welcome and at ease whilst we chatted until I heard a door close and saw Penny the dog come bounding in. She was a small white and tan yappy Jack Russell; not my favourite of dogs, I have to be honest, mostly because they yap. Penny certainly yapped. Incessantly! Then in came Jane: a tall, stocky woman, rather loud-speaking, which was my first impression (well certainly compared to my mum she was). Soon after followed Doug, his father, who was coming back from his shift. I remember immediately feeling more at ease meeting Doug than any of them.

I found him a really genuine and sincere man; my previous thoughts of him couldn't have been more inaccurate. We got all the introductions out of the way and I did at last begin to relax. We chatted about school and my family. His Mum asked lots of questions, wanting to know everything, it seemed. It was getting dark and time for me to leave so I thanked them for having me round and we left together. I came out and felt such relief that I had met them at last. I knew Paul was even happier about it. I admit to feeling as if I was being vetted by his mum, but perhaps that was understandable.

His gran (Doug's mum) lived not very far away from them and I loved her immediately. She was a sweetheart, such a dear, kindly and generous woman, and it soon became apparent that she adored Paul. I could see the feeling was mutual and she was simply delightful. Even up to the year we got married, she left his pocket money on the sideboard and every Saturday he would go to collect it and send us out for cakes from the local bakery, which I learned was as much a weekly and religious tradition as going to church on a Sunday.

Well that was the first meeting over and I admit I began to feel more relaxed, helped by them all being so warm and friendly, although I couldn't help but feel I was being scrutinised by Jane. It continued to feel like this for quite some time, but then I was a serious contender for her youngest son's (her "baby's") affections and I simply had to meet her approval. I felt instantly that his dad liked me, and that helped.

I remember one day in particular that I went with Paul to his house one evening to have tea when his Dad greeted me at the door and said, "I met your mum this morning, wearing a cheeky expression," I was very confused by this and wondered how it could be.

"But you don't know my mum," I said. "You can't have met her." She was at work when I went back earlier and I hadn't seen her myself that day.

"Well let me tell you, I was at the post office on a work visit and she was in the queue. As soon as I saw her, I just knew she was your mum, you look so much like her it was quite incredible. And she is a very attractive lady if you don't mind me saying." At which point he turned to Paul and said, "If you want to know what your wife will look like in years to come then look at her mother. I don't believe you have anything to worry about there!" I blushed like a beetroot, but was also quite touched, if not a little surprised.

As time went by I realised I had been really quite scared of his mum at first, but gradually things settled and I soon began to like her. Over the years, as I began to mature, I learnt to stand up for myself (as was on occasion necessary). I didn't do so in a nasty or confrontational way, but I think as I got older I realised that (perhaps because of the way George had always been towards me) I used to be pushed around a bit by others, particularly at school, where I was frequently bullied. Over time, I learned to stand up for myself. I needed to, as she was very outspoken, honest and to the point. I guess she helped me without me even noticing at the time, as I had always been very quiet and shy.

Paul and I had been courting for almost five years and a wonderful courtship it was. We were both so young, blissfully happy and as I've said earlier, I hadn't really had much experience with boyfriends. There had been the odd date, the occasional kiss, but nothing serious and certainly no one with whom I'd felt any kind of 'connection'. I soon realised I had fallen completely in love and in fact we were both very much in love. Being with Paul felt 'right' somehow, so much so I did in fact refuse the offer of a place to study and become a nursery teacher at Lancaster University. It was something I really did want to do, but I knew I would miss Paul too much to be away for lengthy periods.

One Saturday morning whilst we were together we started talking about buying our first house. We'd already opened a joint bank account a year or so before in the Furness Building Society in order that we could save for a deposit and so that day we decided it was time to start looking to buy.

What an exciting prospect and time this was for us both; buying a house together was a huge commitment to each other but one that we were both most keen to make. This was something very new to Paul and me as both our parents lived on council estates and had never had to deal with mortgages. Nevertheless, we were going to buy a property together, *our* own little house, and live happily ever after. We made an appointment to see the building society, found out how much we could borrow and so the search began.

Well as luck would have it, we bought the first house we'd looked at, a three-bedroom extended terrace. It had the bathroom downstairs beyond the kitchen, which allowed for three bedrooms upstairs. There were two reception rooms; the second one we would use as a sitting-come-dining room, the other one as our lounge. We did view other houses but this was the first one and we had liked it immediately.

It was a bit of a 'project' or perhaps I should say in all honesty a *lot* of a project! It needed almost everything doing to it: wiring, plumbing, decorating, walls knocking through, oh my, the list was endless. But it was lovely, or at least it would be once it was all completed. Most importantly, it was *ours*.

It was all hands on deck once we got the key and work commenced in earnest. Paul was, of course, a plumber so he did all the necessary plumbing, with me as his 'apprentice', fitting sinks and taps, pipe work, even a new boiler. I now know all about hot and cold feeds, traps, flanges, washers, copper piping, flux, pressure valves, u-bends, how to bleed radiators, and, not to forget, tiling and grouting. I helped with it all and admit I did quite enjoy it, well most of the time at least. I did have the odd "sense of humour failure" when I was tired or something wasn't quite right or going to plan. But it was lovely putting our own stamp on our own house.

It also needed a complete total rewire so John, Paul's brother (who incidentally lived in the street behind), did all that. He was helped by Freddy, his brother-in-law, and they replaced every electric cable, power socket, light switch, even new light fittings. In fact everything electrical you could think of. We were most grateful for all their help, as it saved on the expenses, allowing money for the many other needy and imperative jobs.

The removal of the tired and horrid fireplace in the dining room and surrounding brickwork was done by Gags (Grandad, Paul's mum's stepdad) who had come all the way from Barnstaple in Devon, this being where Paul's mum came from herself. Then it was the kitchen, which Paul's dad expertly transformed with fitted kitchen units, all of which he built by hand in his extended brick-built shed in his garden, which came to almost be his second home at times, often to Jane's

73

annoyance. He was originally a pattern maker and clearly a very good one at that; he did a tremendous job, painstakingly building and fitting the kitchen to perfection: a most professional end-result. Last, but not least, all the decoration was completed by my dad and brother, Phillip, something they both excelled at too.

It took almost a year to complete everything and tidy all the mess and mucky jobs, lots of which we did together listening to Duran Duran's new tape *Planet Earth*! We both knew every track off by heart, singing along to it track after track, and dancing around the bedrooms turning up the volume at all my favourite tracks.

Once the mess was done, it was my turn to do what I love and looked forward to most of all, and that was the interior design: choosing colours, fabrics and textiles is something I like to think have a discerning taste for, and something I just love and enjoy doing. It's these last few things that make a house a home and this was *our* home.

Choosing all these beautiful new things together was terribly exciting and fulfilling. That said, he was more than happy for me to take the rein for the most part, as he admitted he didn't have a clue as to such things, and as it was a "woman's job", he was more than happy for me to make final decisions, having now a blank canvas to transform.

The day had come when it was finally finished. We all had worked tirelessly, coming at every available moment to work on our house, and it was beautiful. We were both so very proud indeed of it.

# CHAPTER NINE

One evening we had been out with friends to an end of season football event, as Paul and Kevin, his best friend from school, played Saturday league for The Nautical pub's football team. Whilst he walked me back home, he simply said, "Well I guess we ought to think about setting a date to get married." He was smiling from ear to ear, but seemed a little nervous, I felt.

"Pardon? Am I right in thinking you have you just asked me to marry you?"

"Yes, I guess I have!"

Both of us were smiling now and I said, "Aren't you supposed to get down on one knee at this point?"

"Of course," he said and promptly did just that.

"Yes," I replied, "of course I shall."

Excitedly he took me in his arms, kissed me and said "Gosh. Thank you! I am the happiest man alive." It wasn't quite the romantic proposal I had hoped for or dreamed of but it was a proposal of marriage nevertheless and I was feeling very excited indeed.

We arrived at my house and we decided not to tell anyone as he hadn't got the ring; he wanted me to choose it with him as he insisted it must be just right. He had never bought such an important piece of jewellery; in fact, never before had he bought a piece of jewellery at all. He said it was a big decision and responsibility and he wasn't brave enough to do it himself. I did fully understand that and after all, we were only young. He was just one week exactly older than I was and, at twenty years old, we were young, but very much in love.

He arranged a day out to Bolton to take me to a shop that was said to be the best place to go for such an important purchase and occasion and was heavily advertised on the TV at the time. We left on an early train a few weeks later to get there for the shop's opening and headed straight for Preston's. It was a rather impressive shop, I remember, but sadly also incredibly expensive. I knew the kind of thing I was looking for which was a double diamond on a twist on a gold band, something similar to my mother's which I had always admired.

Mum wasn't a jewellery person at all but always wore her wedding and engagement ring, never ever did she take them off not for any reason. Sadly, they had nothing like it whatsoever, but as Paul quite rightly said it was the first shop we had looked at and we would try elsewhere. Well after a lovely, but rather long day, unsuccessful as regards to the ring, we headed back to the station to come home. I was very disappointed, but remained positive that I would find what I was looking for somewhere.

The following weekend we decided to go into the local town centre and as Paul said there was no harm in looking, so that's what we did. Amazingly, the first jewellers we went in had something very similar to what I had in mind, but with three stones rather than two and it wasn't on a twist. They measured my finger and found they had one left in my size. As soon as I put it on my finger, I simply loved it; it looked perfect, so there and then in a matter of minutes the ring was chosen and bought, and we left the shop smiling and very pleased.

We decided to tell our parents the following day and planned to do it all together and that was exactly what we did: tears of joy were shed, we had a long chat about things and everyone was delighted.

My mum over the coming days had obviously been thinking about this and kindly offered to throw a party for us at the local pub if we waited a few weeks to celebrate it properly, dependent on availability, etc. I was twenty-one the following year and as she had paid for twenty-first birthday parties for the others, but she couldn't afford for me to celebrate both our engagement and my twenty-first so I had to decide which it was to be. We agreed on the engagement and this was planned and paid for over the next few days. We set a date to marry over the following weeks together but decided to keep this decision to ourselves for a little while. It was all so terribly exciting for us both.

I was from a rather large family, certainly compared to Paul's, as my dad was one of eight children and my mum one of six. So Mum decided that once we had told both our parents the news, only immediate family and cousins would be invited to the engagement party in November and aunts and uncles would be invited to the wedding. Mum said they couldn't possibly afford to pay for everyone at both celebrations, and they wanted to do the right thing by everyone. So this was how it was to be.

The evening of the party eventually arrived. We had decided to hold it in one of our local pubs that had a good function room to hire. The room had been decorated beautifully for us. We had a disco booked and food was ordered for eight o'clock in the evening. The guests arrived and Paul met all my cousins, most of them for the first time. We were all having a super time and as Paul stood to invite everyone to help themselves to the food, he announced that I had made him the happiest man in the world by agreeing to marry him, and that the wedding would take place the following September. He didn't want a long engagement; he had made that perfectly clear in conversation before the engagement. The wedding was to be in St Mary's Church on Walney Island, a beautiful church, where he had been a server for many years. The place erupted with cheers and glasses were raised. We had quite the most memorable evening.

We spent the following months organising, arranging and agreeing everything for our wedding, with the help (and in certain cases, interference) from parents. That was to be expected, although at times it could be quite frustrating. It was understood and we just let it all happen.

The guest list was drawn up, the venue was chosen and booked at The Victoria Park Hotel, the menu and costs all agreed with a little guidance from their wedding planner. All the usual protocol was adhered to of course, with suggestions and requests being made by one or another of us. Soon everything was agreed and the deposit paid.

I went with my mum to choose my dress a few weeks later. This was the day I was looking forward to the most (apart from the wedding day) and we had such a wonderful day. We had an appointment at Woodruff's, the only bridal outfitters in the town! We were booked for one pm to view and try on the wedding gowns, so we went for lunch together first and then headed for the shop. I wasn't quite sure on what style I wanted and I didn't want to set my heart on anything too rigid in case I didn't like it when I tried it on. I had a few ideas on what I *didn't* want, but thought I would keep that to myself. So I stuck with my decision to try to go with an open mind as I intended to make the most of the occasion and enjoy every moment.

I introduced myself as we arrived and they were, as I expected, all ready and waiting for us. She escorted us both up to the Bridal Suite situated on the top floor. Once there and seated the assistant went on to ask me if I had any ideas about style, colour, fabric, etc. I said that I didn't as I wanted to come with an open mind and see what they had available, which seemed from her expression to please her. She went on to share from her many years' experience that ladies often ended up disappointed as, for one reason or another they never liked or suited their dream gown. Then began the parade …

I had never seen nor expected the huge choice of dresses and gowns with which I was faced. She continued to show me a countless supply of gowns, some of which I rejected immediately – there is having an open mind but some of these were really awful! There were so many; I did try on some just to please the shop assistant, who was very persuasive, highlighting the fact that I was so slim and young-looking. This seemed to give her the excuse to reveal what I thought was a number of Snow White-themed creations. I felt she was at times treating me almost like a doll.

After two and a half hours of looking and trying on sixteen gowns and various headdresses, I did in fact buy the first one I'd tried on; I knew immediately it was *the one*! This was, of course, confirmed by the tears streaming down my mum's face when she saw me appear wearing it; none of the others had the same effect so my decision was made. I tried it on once more and it undoubtedly confirmed my choice.

It was white and unfussy (certainly compared to some of the horrendous creations I had glimpsed and sensitively rejected) other than for a little Swiss appliqué around the wrist, leading delicately up to my elbow and around the round neckline that trimmed perfectly the sheer yolk and enhanced the sweetheart neckline to the front. It was very elegant indeed and both suited and fitted me perfectly; as the lady said herself it fitted like a glove it seemed the gown had been made to measure. I loved it! Never before had I felt so feminine and elegant.

Pinks and lilacs were my choice of colour for the two bridesmaids' dresses, who were to be my sister and my niece, Michelle. There were, of course, flowers to match and these had to include freesias, as they were my mum's favourite flower. Paul's mum offered to organise these for us as it was her area of expertise; she and her friends from the church would together organise and display the church arrangements so I knew they would be lovely. I'd seen their work displayed there quite often.

Everything was done. Even our Parisian honeymoon was booked with still months to spare. We could now just sit back and excitedly wait for it all to happen, until the day before of course when we knew it would be all systems go, busily rushing here and there ensuring nothing was left to chance so all would go to plan.

# CHAPTER TEN

The day arrived and I went to have my hair and make-up done and go back to spend the last few hours with my parents at 'home'. At least that was the plan: all was going well until Harry came to pick me up from the hairdressers. As soon as we had set off, we were held up in traffic as Walney Bridge had been raised to let the boats through. Why now, of all times? I started to feel panic well and truly setting in. My heart was now racing like a Grand National winner. I really didn't want to be hurried and, more importantly, I promised Paul I wouldn't be late! Thankfully, it was soon lowered and we completed the final few miles at high speed. He actually raced through several red lights to get me home in time, and thankfully one piece. I ran upstairs and began my preparation, albeit more rushed than I had originally hoped and planned for, of course.

My dad called upstairs to announce the arrival of the limousine as I was finishing the last few adjustments to my accessories and spray my perfume. We had chosen a white Rolls Royce; it had been one of Paul's all-time favourite cars so there was no question, that was what it had to be, and it was so perfect.

I descended the stairs to find my father in tears as soon as he saw me. I gave him a cuddle, and then promptly told him to stop; but as he quite rightly pointed out these were our last few moments together at home with me a single woman. "Come on," I said. "You have a very important job to finish here and I don't want any more tears and neither do I want mascara dripping on my beautiful white gown!" I smiled, then wiped his eyes, kissed him gently on the cheek and we left the house. As we opened the door, we were met by a fanfare of cheers, with all our neighbours congregated on the pavement to see us and wave us off. Oh, it was all so wonderfully exciting! I felt like I was in some kind of fairy-tale.

The weather was warm and quite sunny as we slowly made our way. My father didn't want the journey to end and still had tears in his eyes, tears of both joy and sadness, I knew, because he felt he was about to lose me, his baby, his little girl. He held and squeezed my hand so tight I thought he might break it. I gently reminded him he was about to gain a lovely son-in-law, the man I so dearly loved and with whom I wanted to spend the rest of my life, and that he should be happy for me. I didn't really feel I was convincing him at all, but I was sure he would snap out of it once we arrived at the church and he saw everyone inside.

I arrived on time, as promised, at eleven o'clock on Saturday, the fifth of September, 1981. The church bells were joyfully ringing as I stepped out of the car. We walked up the pathway posing for photographs. My Dad was shaking by now and I was beginning to worry he wasn't going to be able to continue, but all was fine once he was out in the fresh air, walking and stopping to talk to all the different people in the crowd, including my cousins that had gathered outside to watch.

The church was full and the flowers looked breathtaking. Suddenly I stopped a moment, glanced directly ahead and I saw him, standing at the altar looking most handsome in a very smart dark grey suit. My heart skipped and butterflies began to make their presence felt within. His brother John, the best man, standing next to him, Paul was wearing the biggest smile and he watched my every step towards him. When I reached him, there were tears in his eyes and said in a slightly nervous voice "Sue, you look beautiful ... really stunning. I am so very proud." He reached for my hand and gently squeezed it.

We were both by now trembling with nerves and a tingling excitement, still gazing longingly into each other's eyes. He winked and we turned to face the vicar for the ceremony to proceed. My father passed Paul my left hand as requested by the vicar and once again, tears drenched his cheeks as he stepped back into the pew to join my mother, who by now was also crying.

The service was so perfect but everything – the hymns, the readings, the vows – all seemed to be over in a heartbeat. He offered his arm, I entwined mine and we walked back down the aisle together, now as husband and wife. Paul looked so incredibly proud, smiling and saying hello to our guests, pausing a moment to speak with those nearest to us on the aisle seats. We were ushered outside for photographs and to be showered with confetti and rice, and a communal roar of congratulations from our guests and well-wishers. A light shower now teased, so we stepped back inside for more photographs.

Once the photographs were completed, the chauffeur led us to the car and opened the door to take us onto to our reception. The venue looked lovely. As is the tradition, we greeted all our guests as they arrived, after which we took our seats. I felt so happy and wildly in love and didn't want the day to end.

The meal was wonderful, accompanied by the murmur and chattering of enjoying *our* day. Alas, it wasn't without a slight mishap, as one of the waiters dropped a bowl of soup in my grandmother's lap. I was unaware at first, but quickly noticed my mother running to her aid, whilst the distraught waiter was led from the dining room. I felt quite sorry for him as it was entirely accidental. My gran was offered a whisky for the shock by the Maître-d'. I had never known her drink, but she accepted and before we knew it a second one arrived. Gran was fine and, despite the embarrassment, she had seemed to revel in the attention.

We had to leave quite early in the afternoon as we were going on honeymoon after the reception and needed to go to the house first to change. Once we were ready, we were driven to the station to catch the four o'clock train to our hotel in London Heathrow, where we were to be staying the night, to be handy to catch our early five o'clock flight to Paris the next morning.

We must have had 'Newlyweds' tattooed on our foreheads because everyone in our carriage was staring and smiling. One woman did actually ask whether it was our honeymoon as we were obviously so happy and in love. We certainly were.

Neither of us had ever flown before so it was a completely new experience for us both. So much so that we almost missed our flight, not knowing about checking the boards, let alone how to find to the required departure gate.

Miraculously we made it with just seconds to spare as we heard the final call, feeling rather flushed, slightly silly and embarrassed as we ran at break-neck speed along the corridors and down the tunnel onto the aircraft, me in my high heels. We boarded and were instantly greeted with laughs and cheeky innuendo from fellow passengers and cabin crew, for it seemed to be obvious to the world that we were dizzy newlyweds.

The flight was very pleasant, but short, which was a shame as I enjoyed every minute (to this day I adore flying). We touched down at Charles De Gaulle airport right on time and to glorious sunshine and a most pleasant and welcoming 22°C, having left the UK at a rather cool 14°C. We took a taxi and headed for our hotel, "The PLM", and checked in.

I was so thrilled and more than a little overcome due to the last twenty-four hours' events. Spending our first night together was going to be different; waking up with him every morning was at first going to feel strange, but it was all so exciting. I can barely remember the first of our five-day honeymoon, and we were having an absolute ball, apart from the food, which I didn't enjoy at all. I simply wasn't used to these ingredients and delicacies, or trying to translate foreign menus. Unfamiliar French cuisine aside, it was the perfect honeymoon and we crammed in and saw as much as possible on the budget we had.

We cruised along the Seine, both during daytime and in the evening to experience and see it in a different perspective of light and atmosphere. We ate at *Le Ciel de Paris* in *Tour Montparnasse*, visited museums and galleries including, of course, the *Louvre*. Upon seeing Da Vinci's *Mona Lisa*, we couldn't help feeling rather disappointed if I'm honest, as it was so much smaller than was expected and the colours somewhat drab. We visited *Notre Dame*, did some shopping and walked and watched a different city breathing. Paris was alive, a most enchanting place to be. I revelled in it all, drinking in the atmosphere. I felt almost childlike again, remembering the boat I saw from the bridge in Barrow, with the glamorous blonde lady gazing out in front.

Overall, we packed a great amount into those few short days and had a truly marvellous, memorable time. It was, of course, the longest time we had ever spent alone together, and it was wonderful. We were both so deeply in love and life was simply perfect. Things surely just couldn't possibly be any better.

We set off back home the following Thursday, leaving sunshine and blue skies, scattered with wisps of white cloud. We arrived into Barrow station to find much cooler temperatures than we had enjoyed in Paris just that morning, and it was of course raining. We didn't care; we just wanted to get home to our beautiful house that we had so lovingly and tirelessly restored into *our* home. We called our parents to let them know that we had arrived safe and sound and that we would enjoy the last few days off work together at home, our virtually new home. And that was exactly what we did.

# CHAPTER ELEVEN

Monday morning came and it was back to work for us both, not something either of us was terribly enthusiastic about, but it had to be done and, as the saying goes, all good things must come to an end. Sadly, the honeymoon was officially now over.

Work was the same old routine; simple but busy. That said I did quite enjoy it, and the company of those around me. We all got on very well, like a big happy family, which was something that the Co-operative society was noted for.

Paul worked as a plumber in Vickers Engineering in Barrow, then more commonly known then as VSEL (or BAE Systems as it is today). The local economy was dominated by manufacturing, in particular shipbuilding and engineering. VSEL was the principal employer for miles around, having traditionally provided jobs for between 12,000 and 13,500 people since 1950. In 1989, the company accounted for a quarter of all local jobs and nearly half of all male employment in the Borough.

Paul served his apprenticeship there, having left school at 16, and was taken on as a permanent employee once his apprenticeship was complete. This was typical and something that was heavily encouraged by parents, fathers in particular, as something that was 'expected' of them. However, Paul's father thought that a plumber was not quite the trade he had hoped for his son at the time. He thought he could have done better, as John his brother was an electrician and that to him was seen as a much better trade to "have under your belt," as he used to say.

Nevertheless, a plumber he was and he did work hard and long hours at times. He also worked overtime to teach an evening class at college, so he was able to earn a bit more, which made things a little easier and allowed us to save a little too.

Then one evening the following July, completely unexpectedly, he came home from work, and, as it was a Thursday, he passed me the Evening Mail, our local rag.

"I've seen a semi-detached house with a garden advertised. Let's make an appointment to view it!" My mouth fell open.

"Why? What about this house – *our* house – and all the work that we've lovingly done to restore it and make it our home?" I was really quite upset at this prospect and so soon after moving in. It had only been ten months, we had lovely neighbours and it was so convenient for shops and family. My head was in a complete spin by now, I just couldn't understand why. We were still getting used to married life and living together here; I just felt it was too soon.

"Where is it?" I asked, as he seemed so keen thought I ought to show a little interest and enthusiasm in his evident excitement.

"Oh, it's only seven doors up on this side of the street. It does look nice. I purposely it passed on my way home to have a look." He was smiling uneasily as I don't think he was expecting my reaction and was a little disappointed. Being so close to where we already lived made it a little easier to consider, so I rather reluctantly agreed to view it. He made an appointment the very next day by calling the private number on the private advertisement in the paper.

The woman that showed us round lived directly opposite the house and, as it turned out, was the daughter of the owner. Her mother had passed away, hence the need to sell the property. She was very nice and seemed friendly and genuine, but I got the definite feeling that she seemed most eager to get rid of it, with no great feeling or emotion about selling the house.

I shared my suspicions with Paul after we had gone back home to discuss our thoughts and feelings about it. He thought this could be a positive thing from the point of possibly getting a good deal and he decided we would put in an offer without haste. I was a little more concerned that there may be something seriously wrong with it, but the survey would or should bring anything like that to light, I guessed.

"How much are we prepared to pay for it?" he asked me. I was in turmoil, my tummy was in knots, and I felt rushed, not to mention sad, about the possibility of leaving my new and lovely home. I came up with a figure, I'm not sure from where, but it felt reasonable and was rather less than the asking price.

This was going to be a *huge* project as it was in need of everything: plumbing, electrics, the windows needed replacing, bathroom refit, and it didn't really have a kitchen. That's not to mention the three large bedrooms, let alone the garden, which was a reasonable size, and that right now was like the proverbial jungle. All this, I felt, more than justified a lower offer. Paul wasn't so sure; he thought we should offer a bit more to try and be more hopeful of securing it, but I refused to start any higher.

The next morning Paul telephoned the woman, put forward our offer and held his breath. He was told she would have to talk to her husband but would ring us back with an answer as soon as she could. I didn't really think they would accept it, if I was honest, but wasn't bothered either way quite frankly! I was also aware, more importantly, that our parents, Paul's in particular, wouldn't be too happy about this news at all. His dad was nervous at the £7000 mortgage we already had; we had paid £8000 for the house and put down a £1000 deposit. We would now need to borrow even more. I also knew he would mention all the hard work that had been put into Number 54 by everyone. I became nervous about telling him, in particular, of all four parents. He was a lovely man, but a real worrier and he couldn't help but express his opinion at times, especially when it came to financial matters. He wasn't going to like this one little bit.

About an hour later, the phone rang and I answered. It was the woman to say, much to our astonishment, that they would accept the offer. I passed the good news to Paul who was delighted. On reflection, it did seem a good deal and it would be nice once all the work was complete. I just had to keep telling myself that as I dreaded the thought all that hard work again, and so soon, and with a bigger mortgage. It would take even longer to do as it was a bigger house and with a garden, that was nothing but a jungle, with only a stunted lilac tree in the bottom corner. Worse still, this time we were going to have to live in it whilst all the work was done.

However, the thought of having a garden was one thing I really liked. Moreover, it was a semidetached and was in a nice position in the street; being on the highest point it had a better view and benefitted from a slightly larger front garden than others close by. Gradually I was coming round to the idea, and Paul was doing everything to convince me it was the right decision. As ever, he won me over. He clearly 'wore the trousers' when it came to financial matters, rather like his own father. So it all began once more.

# CHAPTER TWELVE

Our house was sold before it even went on the market. The evening after we'd spoken to the estate agent, there was a knock at the door and when I opened it a young woman and her husband, both of whom I thought I recognised, were standing in front of me.

"I feel a little cheeky but I hear the house is for sale. Can I come in and have a look around please?" she asked. To say I was rather taken aback was an understatement but nonetheless agreed. She stood in the hall, looked in at the lounge from the hallway and a torrent left her mouth: "I love it! We want it! I heard from my mum, who'd been talking to Glenys, her neighbour – my cousin – today and thought I best not leave it as I heard how beautiful it was, it all then fell into place, so how much do you want?"

The estate agent had been that afternoon and valued it at £13,250, which we'd been delighted about of course, but I replied with £13,750. She shook my hand: "OK it's a deal, thank you!" and they promptly left. They hadn't even seen it, any of it, but a deal had been done and an easy sale for the agent.

Delighted at the simplicity of the whole process so far convinced me, to coin a phrase my mum often used, that "it was meant to be." Paul was amazed at my cheek and sudden enthusiasm. Within twenty-four hours, we had bought and sold a property, but forty-eight hours ago, I'd had no idea that any of this was even a consideration.

It was all systems go now as our buyer wanted to move in within, six weeks' time and were first time buyers. The house we were buying was empty, but for an old kitchenette unit she had left, which was fortunate as it had little else in the way of space. The woman just wanted it sold and kindly offered that we could begin the work before its completion. She liked the look of us; we seemed honest and trustworthy. Not something I would recommend today, but it certainly helped at the time. She did go on to say that she would be delighted to see it restored and lived in once again, although when I found out that her mother had actually died in the one of the bedrooms it rather spooked me.

It's fair to say that the news, as expected, did NOT go down at all well with Paul's dad. We had lectures and frequent visits to the house, reminding us of all the hard work everyone had ploughed into Number 54. Not to mention the mortgage! I do admit to wondering if he might be right, he certainly did have a point about the mortgage. However, whatever happened, he was going to have to accept what we were doing; after all, we were married adults and it was our business. It took a little while, but he did understand ... eventually. I was gradually getting used to him and his worrying ways, but it wasn't easy at times.

After the usual delays and painstaking heel-dragging, with solicitors picking over a few minor things, we moved into Number 76 ten weeks later. The realisation of everything that needed to be done suddenly became even more apparent. I started to feel very uncomfortable and 'out of place'. We closed the front door, having finished unloading everything and began the arduous task of unpacking the mass of boxes, starting in the kitchen, such as it was.

The woman had left all the curtains up (such as they were with moth eaten holes) but at least it meant we didn't have to worry about being too exposed – one thing less to do for the moment. She also she left all the light bulbs so we had lights throughout (when we moved into Number 54 we had only one bulb, which meant we had to keep taking out and plugging it back in to view each room). We didn't dare even try the huge ancient storage heaters, so temporarily resorted to the ugly electric fire in the hearth, expensive as it would be to run. There was no gas in the house at all so that was going to be interesting, not to mention costly.

I was feeling a complete mix of emotions and felt the need go into the bathroom to shed a tear or two in private. I wanted so much to stay positive for Paul's sake and I didn't want to cry in front of him. I did really believe it would all be worth it in the end; it was that getting there was going to be another very long and messy road and this time we had to live amongst it all. I was already missing my lovely hand-built-with-love kitchen and new carpets; especially the lovely hall and stairs one that was kindly paid for by Paul's amazing Gran who lived a few streets away.

Somehow, we pressed on day-to-day and, when we had been in for almost a year; some of the rooms were starting to take shape at last. We had had gas installed; Paul and his friend, Kevin, who worked for the gas board, did all of this together, including (as the very first job) installing a new combi boiler to give us instant constant hot water. Next, we got a builder friend to knock down a wall in the kitchen and block out one of the two doors into the lounge. He also moved the back door from the side of the house to the back to open onto the back garden and have the effect of extending the kitchen. It also allowed for extra wall and floor space for the much-needed units.

Next, we had the bathroom ripped out and replaced with a pampas-coloured suite (the latest colour at the time!). Of course, Paul did this, with me as his labourer! Gags came around as they were here on holiday from Barnstaple and he kindly fully tiled the walls; he said it would keep him out of mischief and from under Gran and Mum's feet, and leave them to do 'girl stuff'. Gran was more than happy for him to help us and it looked fabulous when it was all finished,

Dad was making new windows for us now, lovely mahogany ones they were. We had a quote for UPVC windows but these came in most expensive. We couldn't afford them so Dad kindly offered to make them all for us. He had mellowed a little by now and, as hard as it was for him, he did admit that it had been a good move; he apologised for his lack of enthusiasm and the lectures, but stressed that it was only because he cared. He really liked the house, I could tell, but he was reluctant to admit it for a while.

This time we bought the kitchen units as I had seen a range I liked in a local kitchen showroom; they were in the sale, which was an advantage amidst all the expense of everything. I really liked them and luckily, they were exactly what I had in mind. The kitchen as well as being small tended to be a little dark, especially in the afternoon, so I wanted them to be light in colour and I knew these would fit the bill perfectly.

We chose a linen colour with an oak trim and worktops that matched beautifully. Paul fit an oak tongue and groove ceiling with chrome sunken lights, and we chose contrasting tiles to finish it all off. I say "we", although I did most of the decision making when it came to fittings and furnishings; Paul often said I had a keen eye for such things and always chose well. Having a blank canvas to work with and transform was a most exciting and pleasing project for me. Paul often thought interior design was something I should have seriously considered as a career and was something in which I particularly revelled.

The kitchen and bathroom were a priority and the biggest jobs where most work was needed, and, of course, all the mess that went with it. Once they were done, though, it was the bedrooms. Our bedroom was started first and we had already decided to have fitted floor-to-ceiling sliding robes with glass doors as the room had a huge alcove that simply screamed out for them I thought. We did accept Dad's kind help again with these, as it was without doubt a two-man job; they were heavy, very fiddly to hang, and ensuring the runners ran straight was imperative. Paul had never done anything like this before.

It took them about a week to finish as Dad also fitted built-in shelves and drawers inside one section of it. This would help keep things tidy and out of the way, as well as to make use of the large space they filled. It would also save buying a chest of drawers that would take up limited floor space, as it was not the biggest of bedrooms. As ever, he did a great job. I now really couldn't wait to get our clothes put away and on hangers at last.

I was very lucky having lovely in-laws as a number of my friends and colleagues unfortunately didn't – some didn't even speak to each other. I simply could never imagine that.

Dad (that is, Paul's dad) was in the Royal Horseguards from his late teens, and that was how he met Mum; she was a nanny to the Royal family at Windsor Castle. They had met at a dance, and had a rather romantic courtship as I was told; it all sounded so fairy-tale, and in truth, I think it was. They eventually married in Windsor (not the castle but a sweet little church not a stone's throw from it). Between the two of them, they had some very interesting stories, Mum especially, of certain 'below stairs' antics and goings on, none which of which I could possibly disclose here!

Dad eventually left the Horseguards when they married and joined the police as a constable, which also provided their home, a job that he did for the rest of his working life. He never was at all ambitious to move onwards or upwards with his career, neither did he consider doing anything else. Motivation and aspiration were non-existent but he was happy.

He did, however, once have the opportunity to inherit his parents' beautiful house in Swarthmoor some years earlier, just months before I met Paul, but he didn't want it as he saw it as lots of hard work, a never-ending project. It was a rather large property with outbuildings and a large greenhouse, all set in large grounds. I always thought it a terrible shame that he didn't want it and wondered if it would be something he would later come to regret as it was such a delightful property. He clearly was more than capable of handling it but you can't force people to do things they don't want to – you can lead a horse to water but you can't make it drink.

Paul's mum never really worked once she left Windsor and moved to Barrow, other than a part-time cleaning job to pass a few hours in the local public house. Instead, she concentrated on bringing up the boys and being a devoted Mum and housewife. She never had a daughter, but that was a role I eventually managed to fill. We got on very well indeed and became very close; we could talk about anything and were always there for each other. Naturally, we had a few minor issues, but never anything serious at all. She often referred to me as her daughter whenever she introduced me publicly to anyone, and I can honestly say I felt like it. I was indeed very lucky and proud to have her as my mother-in-law and I love her very much.

Paul's brother's wife was a very different person and personality to me in every way. We were two complete opposites, and her relationship with Mum was completely different to mine. They got on well but we were very different people with different personalities and very different opinions on many things. They lived a very insular life, but that was their business and it wouldn't do for us all to be the same.

It took almost two years to finish with Number 74, but at last it was all done. We had actually finished, well almost, with the exception of the garden and that could certainly wait a while. Mum wanted to help with this and she certainly knew her plants very well having done a beautifully colourful job with her own gardens, not to mention flower arranging in the church at the weekends. We agreed to do it all together over the coming weekends and the first job would definitely be digging up the huge sickly lilac tree in the bottom corner. Paul's mum and I both agreed to replace it with a beautiful copper beech, one of my favourite trees. My favourite of them is the weeping willow; I hope that one day, in the not too distant future, one shall proudly adorn my garden.

# CHAPTER THIRTEEN

We had been married for almost three years and my maternal instincts were kicking in big time. We had discussed having children on many occasions, and I often dreamt of having a baby, and making what I believe one of the biggest and important commitments a couple can make. I love children and did come to regret not taking my place as a nursery teacher at Lancaster University when I left school; but we were in love and simply couldn't bear the thought of being apart so I declined the opportunity.

We had been so busy renovating two houses that, along with all the cost involved, meant that the time hadn't been right until now. We talked about it seriously and agreed that we would start trying but wouldn't get hung up over it and things would, God willing, take their course. We both agreed that we would like three children, but one step at a time.

I awoke one morning a few weeks later feeling 'different'. I couldn't quite put my finger on why I wasn't quite feeling myself; I didn't feel ill but neither did I feel quite right. I decided it would pass in a day or so and just convinced myself it was a viral infection. Three days later, I was fine and back to normal, more or less. I had obviously caught something; nothing too serious or to worry about and it hadn't kept me from work.

The following week I was making a cup of tea and I couldn't drink it; the very smell as I put it to my mouth turned my stomach. I am a true Northerner and love a cup of tea, but I felt green. This was silly, I thought, and so I attempted to try another one again a little later but the same feeling came over me. This definitely wasn't right and that morning I remembered feeling a little nauseous. Something was wrong so I thought I would go and see the doctor; maybe something was lingering around from the virus I guessed I had.

I went after work and saw Dr Todd. I sat down in his surgery, he asked me a few questions and as soon as I told him my symptoms he smiled and passed me a container across the table; I was to take a urine specimen first thing the next day and drop it into reception. He said that I was probably pregnant and this would prove it either way. I couldn't believe it; I must have fallen pregnant immediately. Looking back at all the different feelings in the previous week or so, it did all start to make sense, but I decided to stay calm and wait to call surgery three days later for the results. Oh, what a long three days it was.

I tried to keep calm and collected but just wanted to know. I rang promptly at eleven o'clock, as that was when the results were going to be available. I composed myself and prepared for disappointment, but thankfully was told the results were positive. Tears of joy streamed down my cheeks; I just couldn't believe how lucky we were. I went home to ring Paul to share our news, as I simply couldn't wait to tell him to his face.

I was pregnant *already*. I was having a baby, our baby. My wonderful husband and I were going to be parents. I couldn't wait any longer to tell him and needed to share our fantastic news. He had a right to know now and so I made the call and simply said, "You're going to be a Daddy!" I could actually *hear* him smiling; I knew he was grinning like the proverbial Cheshire cat. I could see his face and he was three miles away at work!

"Really? That's fantastic news," he said. "I love you, Sue … I am so pleased and proud."

He came home at lunchtime and we first went to my parents to tell them. After tea, when his dad would be in for his meal break, we went to tell them both also. We wanted to tell them all face to face and, as expected, there were tears of joy, congratulations and pure elation from both sets of parents.

I went to see the doctor the following week for examinations and questions and was given an expected date of 2$^{nd}$ February (1984). Paul's birthday is 29$^{th}$ January and mine is 5$^{th}$ February so perhaps the baby would may even arrive on one of our birthdays and give us a truly wonderful present.

As pregnancies go, I do believe I had a very good and easy one. I continued for a few weeks with slight bouts of nausea but never was actually sick. I couldn't drink tea for the first few months at all or even be in the kitchen while one was being made; I just couldn't bear the smell, so I took to drinking water and juice. I considered myself very lucky indeed, particularly as a friend of mine the previous year was sick every single day of her entire pregnancy; she was in and out of hospital as they were very concerned for her and the baby, although fortunately all was fine in the end.

I was sent for a scan as the doctors thought I was rather large for my term; also, as there were twins in the family on Paul's side (his grandmother was a twin and they say they skip a generation) so that was a possibility. After the scan I was relieved to be told there was just one, although they did find that the baby was breach. They thought there was plenty of time for it to turn and that I was not to worry, but when I went back for my next appointment they decided they would have to turn it themselves there and then. It was not a pleasant experience, but they did it and were happy that it had been successful.

We were in bed later that evening and I was unusually in a restful slumber, laid on my side against Paul's back; this made a welcome change as when baby had been breach its head was in such a position as to make it impossible to get comfortable in my usual position. I woke suddenly with a most strange sensation. Paul jumped and turned quickly to look at me: "I felt that. What was it? Are you OK?" Oh no, the baby had turned back again I could feel the head there under my ribs once again.

I was only a few weeks away from my expected date now and they were keeping a close eye on me as my blood pressure had started to rise a little; they weren't too worried but decided to send the midwife out to me daily just to keep a check on things till the baby came. Jane, the midwife, was nice and I knew her from school. She arrived just before lunchtime one Thursday two weeks before the expected arrival date and took my blood pressure, I was lying on the sofa; she looked at me after seeing the reading and told me off as it was very high, dangerously high. She said she was going to have to admit me to hospital immediately and that I should contact Paul to let him know.

She knew I didn't want to go in, but was having none of my gentle persuasion; she was simply doing her job, as I knew (having been reading up on it) that both the baby and I could be in danger if I stayed at home. Jane did agree, however, that Paul could take me in if I managed to contact him whilst she was there with me, otherwise I had to be taken by ambulance; she gave me strict orders to be at the hospital within the hour. Paul, of course, came home immediately; I broke down when he came through the door and I fell into his arms sobbing. He was clearly very concerned, I could see, and he tried to reassure me and agreed that it was the best place for me to be, for both the baby's safety and mine. He then gathered my things together and off we went by taxi. I was in my hospital bed by two o'clock and told I was on complete bed rest; I wasn't even allowed to get out to pee – I had to use a bedpan, which is no easy thing to undertake.

I had almost two weeks still to go until the due date so prayed that over the next few days things would settle down and they would let me home. Sadly, this was not to be and I was still there on 7th February, two weeks later. My blood pressure had dropped a little, not nearly enough for me to be discharged, and neither was I showing any signs of starting labour. The doctor came to see me on his rounds that morning and even came back that evening to see how I was doing. There were no signs of anything happening at all, not even a twinge or any other signs of labour.

The doctor decided that he would ring the ward the following morning, as he was on leave, and that if there were no signs of movement he would take me down to theatre to perform a caesarean section in the afternoon. I was mortified at the prospect and of course wanted to give birth naturally; I was so worried and upset that I eventually cried myself to sleep.

The next morning I had to be woken up, a wonderful change, as sleeping for any length of time with so much activity around, bells and buzzers going off, people shouting or crying, dreaming or snoring, sleeping was virtually impossible. I was told I couldn't eat anything due to the impending operation, but I didn't care about food; I just wanted to hold our baby and to go home and sleep in our bed. I had been in hospital for two weeks and missed Paul very much; they were very strict at visiting hours and I had to be kept calm and rested because of the blood pressure.

The nurse came to see me around ten o'clock, said the doctor had called in and as there was still nothing happening they had scheduled the section for one o'clock that afternoon. She gave me an enema, which, although necessary, was most an unpleasant and undignified experience. She then went on to say that I could call Paul to tell him and that he could come to see me before the operation and stay with me until they took me into theatre when he would be asked to sit close by in a side bay until it was all over. Hallelujah! It was finally happening and I could barely believe it.

Paul arrived at twelve-thirty and sat with me, holding my hand. We were both feeling a mixture of emotions by now but I could tell that he was very worried but was trying hard to hide it by keeping me quietly occupied with calm conversation. He knew this wasn't how I had hoped it would be, but, of course, the safety and security of our baby and me was of paramount importance. The duty nurse came and told him he had to leave me, so he lent down to kiss me and said goodbye in an excited but concerned voice. "See you and our baby in a little while," he said, as they pushed me into theatre.

I remember stirring, hearing my name being called and realising it was the nurse who was stroking my hand and trying to wake me. I blearily made eye contact with her and tried to ask whether I'd had a boy or a girl, but it came out complete nonsense. She realised what I was asking but shook her head and said with a big smile that she couldn't tell me, as Paul wanted to be the privileged bearer of that news. She was a lovely nurse who had taken a few of the antenatal classes we'd attended and we hit it off. She promised that she would be at the birth with me come what may and she had kept to her word. She had even come in to work on her day off to be with me.

I dropped back off to sleep and remember waking again with a start and feeling dreadful; I drifted in and out of consciousness and felt so ill. I was by then, I gathered, back on a different ward when I turned to see Paul on my left holding our baby. He gave me quite the biggest smile, like the one I'd imagine he had when I'd told him on the phone that I was pregnant, and then bent down to kiss me: "We have a Sarah, look." He had our baby, Sarah, in his arms, looking so proud. He'd liked the name all through the pregnancy; someone at church he had met some years ago had the name, and he asked me then if we had a girl whether we could call her Sarah. We both pored over loads of name books but Sarah stuck and I loved it too; we could never agree on a boy's name, so it was just as well she was pink.

He tried to put her carefully in the crook of my left arm but I couldn't take her; I was drifting away again and was feeling strange, very sick and very sore. I was willing myself to wake up and hold both her and my husband but I drifted off again. I carried on like this for what seemed forever when I heard an alarm sound very near. One of the sisters came rushing over and tried to talk to me; she was shouting my name anxiously and tapping my face. She physically turned my head to look at her and she was trying to ask me to tell her what was wrong and how I was feeling. I just couldn't get any words out and was just starting to sense that there was a serious problem when once again I was out cold.

I opened my eyes once more; it must have only been for seconds that I had been unconscious, but it felt like an eternity and she was still looking down at me. "Susan!" she shouted. "I really need you to talk to me and tell me what's wrong. Please don't go back to sleep." She was shaking my arm and I tried to shrug my shoulders but still couldn't get a single word to leave my lips. She then threw the sheet off me, looked down, and screamed for a doctor. She began to push gently down on my tummy and I remember feeling this most unpleasant warm and wet sensation gushing from my lower abdomen; I was haemorrhaging. Suddenly there was utter pandemonium all around me. I heard her say, "We are losing her," when her voice trailed off once more.

I awoke again now with a doctor either side of me and the sister at my feet, looking at the evacuation I had just released. There was another nurse trying to fit a blood pressure cuff to my left arm and someone I didn't know standing at my head behind me with their hands on my shoulders. I turned to the nurse at my arm and managed from somewhere to find a slight voice, and whispered, "Am I going to live to see my baby? Am I? Please tell her I am sorry and that love her and to be happy." I started to drift off again although I could feel my heart pounding and my head felt ready to explode. I was aware of being lifted as they transferred me to a gurney trolley and proceeded to wheel me at high speed out of the ward and down the corridor. I don't remember much after that; once again I was out cold.

# CHAPTER FOURTEEN

I heard voices in the distance and aware that someone was touching my hand, I began to stir. I had the headache from hell and felt so week and trembling. A nurse was taking my blood pressure once again; her face was hazy but I heard her gentle voice. "Hello, Sue, welcome back," she said with a sweet smile. I desperately needed a drink of water and my mouth felt as dry as sand. The nurse asked how I was feeling and I told her about my head but I desperately needed a drink of water. She then stuck a sponge on a stick in my mouth and said to suck that as I she couldn't let me have a proper drink just yet, as the anaesthetic still in my body would make me vomit.

I heard footsteps coming towards my room and turned to see Paul looking rather jaded; he stroked my head and bent to kiss me. "How are you? I have been so worried – in fact you had us all very worried for a while." I was in a single side room; I didn't like it, not at all. I felt very uneasy, as I knew that a Mum had lost her baby in this very room the previous night. I heard her haunting screams and could almost feel her tears sting my eyes; I felt so desperately sorry for her. I began to panic, my heart now racing and wanted to see my baby. I began to cry, fearing the worst. Paul held me tight. "Don't worry, Sarah's fine. She's in the nursery being fed as you were otherwise engaged! They'll bring her through in a little while."

"What time is it?" I asked. It was just after seven in the evening. I couldn't believe that they had taken me down so long ago. I had been out of it all afternoon. A squeaky trolley approached and a nurse entered my room smiling cheerily.

She passed Sarah to Paul from the cot and then he said, "At last let me introduce you to our beautiful daughter. We have a Sarah!" With that lovely smile, again he put her gently into the crook of my left arm. She was beyond beautiful; weighing 8lb 7oz and seventeen and a half inches long, with a shock of very dark hair and rather olive skin, big blue eyes and the cutest little mouth. She was simply perfect, and having been delivered by caesarean, she was flawless.

I held her in my arms and couldn't take my eyes off her; I was telling her how much I loved her and that I'd never been so proud in my life, but I was also sad that I had missed her first few hours of life. Tears of joy were slipping down my cheeks. Then once again, I suddenly came over very weak and lethargic and sensed a warm feeling between my legs again. I thought I had wet myself so turned and said to Paul, "Can you take her? I'm afraid I'm going to drop her. I don't feel very well." When I looked down, I was bleeding once again.

He shouted for the nurse who came straight away. She did all the necessary OB/GYNs and injected more painkillers in my left thigh – I was beginning to feel like a pincushion by now. I lay down flat and could feel myself drifting away once more. The nurse had said for Paul to go into the waiting room once again or to go on home and they would contact him if there was a problem. The nurse put Sarah Jane in her cot by my bedside and told Paul to try not to worry.

The next I knew it was around eleven thirty in the evening. I had been very restless and had had numerous visits from different doctors and nurses and, although I was feeling a little more with it, I was still very unhappy about being in this room. I asked if I could get out of bed to go to the bathroom; the nurse agreed and seemed very pleased that I was asking to go, but I was not allowed to go on my own so she happily assisted me.

I thought her a friendly and gentle nurse and I had learned already from my stay in hospital that there a few who certainly were not. It seemed that some had never heard of 'good bedside manner', but this nurse was very caring and kind and accompanied me as I shuffled gingerly to the bathroom. I asked about moving to the open ward but she said I wasn't allowed to as they had to keep a close eye on me. I'd encountered a few problems and was not quite out of the woods, but they would see how was in the morning.

I hoped to be moved after breakfast but it would be the doctor who would make that decision. She assured me that he would be made aware of my request, and more importantly, why I was making it. Breakfast? Food was the last thing on my mind; I had no appetite whatsoever.

Sarah Jane was in the nursery and was hungry so they brought her to me to feed her; breast feeding was not something I was very confident or comfortable about but I was determined to try it at least; "breast is best," as they say, but Paul and I naturally wanted that for her if I could possibly do it. She was certainly a hungry girl and quite demanding, although I did seem to manage to feed her, so I felt a bit happier about the task.

The following morning the doctor did his rounds and came to talk to me, as at least I was by now compos mentis. He was of average build and height with sandy coloured hair and lovely bluish, almost grey coloured eyes. They were very striking and many women (me included) would envy him for them. He had a lovely bedside manner and spoke very gently; Mr Arman was quite a religious man, generally very much against caesarean births and would avoid the procedure if he possibly could. C-sections were very much a last resort option in his eyes, which was partly why he kept me hanging on as long as he did.

I had been in for two weeks on the day I had Sarah, but my blood pressure was still of such concern that he reluctantly decided to perform the caesarean, despite the risks. He admitted that I had given them all a hairy, scary twenty-four hours as I had been in an almost critical condition; a culmination of toxaemia, high blood pressure, a bad reaction to the anaesthetic, haemorrhaging and vomiting. Overall, giving birth for me was not proving the experience I had anticipated at all. In fact, I was urged to seriously consider whether to have another baby, but for now that was the last thing I wanted to think about.

Dr Arman went on to say he was happy that I was showing good signs of improvement; I had to stay calm and stress free my blood pressure would have to be regularly monitored. Once I was eating, drinking and going to the bathroom normally he would allow me to go back to the open ward.

The doctor was very happy with Sarah but the paediatrician would like to come to take a thorough look at her later that morning, as is normal with all new-born babies. He went on to say that when they'd delivered her, her right leg had been bent backwards which, had I tried to give birth naturally, would undoubtedly have caused great problems. They did need to ensure there were no problems with her leg or hip because of her position in the womb. He smiled, rose from his chair and as he left the room said he would call back to check my progress before he finished his shift later that afternoon.

I had been pleased with the doctor's assessment of Sarah as I was beginning to think some of the nurses were in the secret service; they wouldn't tell me anything, with the exception of Katy the previous night, although even she hadn't given much away. However, I began to get rather anxious about what the paediatrician would say about Sarah's situation. It was rather uncanny, as when Paul had been born, his toes had been attached to his shin because of his length and position in the womb, hence my increased concern.

At eleven o'clock, the paediatrician came round and examined Sarah, mostly in her cot beside me, but he did say he needed to take her away for a little while to carry out a further test and get a second opinion on her hip. Anxiously I agreed and he wheeled her cot out of the ward. I was so worried with tears welling up as I imagined all kinds of problems, while at the same time worrying about keeping my blood pressure under control. Then, about fifteen minutes later, he returned with her smiling.

"All is fine, Mrs Barker. Nothing at all to worry about, I was just being thorough in case she had a slight hip disorder as a result of the leg position in the womb. But it's all fine, I assure you." With that, he left.

I reached over and lifted her from the cot to cuddle her and talk to her, and of course to feed and change her; she was always hungry. I popped her back into the cot after she'd fallen asleep in my arms and walked to the bathroom, expecting the wrath of the duty nurse for not calling for assistance; but I managed it alone and once back in bed I asked for something to eat and a cup of tea. The nurse was delighted to oblige and within ten minutes, I had it delivered and eaten with only crumbs left on the plate; it was the best piece of toast I had ever eaten for sure. She then brought my menu for the evening meal as I seemed to be on a bit of a roll now and she was keenest to encourage my appetite.

The doctor came back, as promised, later that afternoon. It was just before four o'clock and, having already woken from a lovely slumber, I was feeling much more lucid. He made a few enquiries with the duty nurse at his side and looked at my chart and said to me, "I am pleased to see that you have accomplished my earlier requests successfully," in a rather droll tone I might add, "and I am now happy that you can move to the other ward. The porter will be notified to come for you as soon as he is available." Oh, I could have hugged him; I was so pleased. I wanted so much to get out of that dreadfully morbid room. I'd prayed that I wouldn't have to spend another night in there. I had my meal brought and had finished it all so that by six o'clock we were both back in my original ward, but nearer the door this time. Sarah Jane was fast asleep beside me, completely oblivious to it all.

I suddenly felt so much better and more relaxed. I remembered Chris, the woman in the bed next to me from when I was admitted; she lived not too far from me, as it had turned out in conversation, although I didn't recognise her from the Island. She had, just two hours earlier, delivered her sixth girl, who she also named Sarah (spelt Sara). No boys! She had all girls, but she was very happy. If I'm honest, I had always secretly wanted a girl and I couldn't believe how lucky I had been.

The next few days were OK but I sensed something still wasn't quite right with Sarah Jane. I didn't know quite what, but she was just so hungry that now even the doctor on the fourth day was becoming concerned with her losing weight; as they discovered she had lost almost two pounds of her birth weight when they had weighed her in the early evening. They then decided to attach me to a machine (which the nurses called Daisy Dairy!) to extract my milk and bottle it for her. It was by doing this they realised that my right breast wasn't releasing milk as it should; in fact it was proving difficult to extract much from it at all.

Luckily, from this discovery they deduced the problem was due to a blockage, which meant that Sarah was getting only half her feed, poor little girl, was no wonder she was constantly hungry and upset. On the face of it, this was most surprising, as my boobs were huge at 42DD! I am sure I must have looked like a Weeble (a child's toy from the 1970s that wobbled but didn't fall down) Normally measuring 34C, standing 5'5" tall and size 12 (pre-pregnancy) it felt very odd indeed; I liken it to carrying around the Rock of

Gibraltar times two, and that was far from pleasant I can assure you.

Paul had left as visiting time had finished a few hours previously, so I asked for the portable phone to be brought to the bed (no such luxury as mobiles then). I called him, told him what they'd said and asked if he would mind her having bottled milk, as I wanted it to be a joint decision, as it seemed it was best for our daughter and me. That was it; bottles from there on and I didn't regret it. "Breast is best," was almost forced upon you but it isn't possible for everyone, even if they want to do it. Sarah started to gain weight almost immediately with the bottled milk, supplemented with my milk. The nurses extracted my milk daily with the "milking machine", something that became something of a joke between the nurses and me.

A week later, the doctor asked whether I wanted to go home. It was just music to my ears: my blood pressure was almost normal (136/88), my wound was healing nicely and Sarah was quite simply perfect, almost back to her birth weight and so content she was like a different baby. I was so happy now and her Daddy was elated as he couldn't wait to have us both home at last. He arrived immediately to escort us home, and we waited a little while for an available nurse to carry her out of the hospital; back then, parents were not permitted to do so and babies had to be officially handed over at the door. Nonetheless, our lives as new parents could now begin at home.

# CHAPTER FIFTEEN

Within half an hour, we were home at last. Everything felt very different now; I'd left the house in tears almost a month ago and a great deal had happened in that time, plenty of which I remember very little about, but I was now feeling that had maybe been for the best. I stepped back inside a mother, a very proud mother at that, and Paul, it was evident, was equally delighted and proud at becoming a father.

I went upstairs very gingerly, as I had been given strict instructions before leaving the hospital on the entire "do's and don'ts" at home: no hoovering, stretching, lifting, not even the kettle, as all the internal healing would take some time to mend. If I overdid anything, it might cause more internal damage or bleeding, as they had to cut me more than they had hoped. Things then were so different then to today.

I walked into her room to see the new finished nursery with the Beatrix Potter wallpaper that we had chosen; it had a soft, lemon background with all the characters in soft tones and smiling faces. We had the matching curtains, a new light fitting and Paul had put together her new mahogany cot. He'd placed some soft toys inside and had left all the bedding ready for me to make it up for her as he knew I'd want to do that. Oh, it all looked so pretty and perfect for our little girl. I was so pleased with it all – he had done us proud.

I was beginning to feel very tired, something that I had come to accept. I was willing and wanting to do so much but was just not able to and it did become most frustrating over the next month or so. I am not, nor have I ever been, a lazy person, always on the go doing something or other, but this operation had undoubtedly highlighted my limitations, at least for the moment.

Sarah settled immediately into her new room and from day one, she was no bother at all; she was growing more beautiful by the day. I became stronger and after my six-week check-up I was given a clean bill of health; I just had to take thing sensibly for a few more weeks but I was feeling great and almost back to normal.

As the months passed we got into our routine without any great problems. She started to walk just before her first birthday and she was dry in no time; she never could bare a wet nappy, which helped make the dry stage even easier to achieve.

I didn't go out to work until she started school and then it was part time to coincide with school hours so I could take her there myself and pick her up afterwards. I wanted to stay at home to be a full-time Mum; children are only young once and I didn't want to miss any of it if I could help it: her saying her first word and taking her first step. I wanted to be there for her and for me, not that you can guarantee you will witness these things, but being there full time must give you a much better chance. I am very proud to say that I was.

# CHAPTER SIXTEEN

Before we had Sarah, I had always expected that by the time our first child had reach around two years old, we would have possibly been preparing to start trying for our second baby, as originally we wanted three children. No matter what I thought or how I looked at the possibility, however, I just couldn't get past the last weeks of my pregnancy, the difficult birth and the post-op problems that ensued in the weeks following the birth.

I also suffered from awful post-natal depression when she was almost a year old. My doctor at the time wouldn't have it at all; he thought it was ridiculous as she was almost a year old. Paul didn't want to come to the GP with me at first; he thought I should just pull myself together and seemed to take my condition quite personally.

I think over the years it is a condition has been quite understated, well at least it was then. However, I can assure you that it certainly does exist and is a dreadful condition to suffer: waking up feeling so dark, worthless and tired, a great lack of self-esteem, being constantly tearful and feeling alone and worthless, to name but a few symptoms. It was horrid.

My mum, when I visited her one morning, found me in tears on the doorstep as she opened the front door. She immediately called the doctor and made an appointment for me to see him straightaway. At last, the doctor accepted that I was depressed and was most concerned at the time, needing some reassurance that I wasn't about to throw myself under a bus on my way home. I half-laughed at the question at first until I was realised he really meant it. After a time I came through it, but it was a truly awful experience and pregnancy sadly became a tremendous fear for me; I was simply terrified at the sheer thought of it. Not that Paul and I abstained at all from sex, we had a very full love life, but it was also with precautions.

I knew Paul would still have loved another baby and that didn't help me either as I felt terribly guilty. I think if someone had dropped our second baby in my lap, that would have been perfect, but, of course, that's silly and not how it works. Therefore, I decided that I would go to see my doctor and discuss my concerns, as I was also now becoming rather down about the whole situation and it was beginning to worry me. The situation was not helped by people saying how unfair it would have been to have an only child, or asking me whether I was pregnant again. "Oh, she needs a baby brother or sister now," and, "an only child is a lonely child." These were not helpful remarks at all.

I went to discuss it alone with the doctor. He listened carefully to my fears and concerns, read the notes from my time in hospital and concluded that a second child was not a good idea at this stage. He helped me try to think differently and more positively about not having a second baby, although finished by adding that, as I was still young, I might change my mind in the future.

I came out with mixed emotions; I was happier with his words and support, but also rather sad as it finally confirmed things. It was almost as if I needed his blessing in some way to justify my reasons. Motherhood for me was more than likely over. Having just one baby was not in our ideal plans, but then Sarah was *the* best baby anyone could have. I consoled myself by constantly reminding myself of that, and of how proud and lucky we were to have her. Even at that time, I was sadly more than aware that there are people far less fortunate than Paul and I.

I did have a pregnancy scare once but thankfully it was a false alarm; my fear and anxiety at the time proved more than ever to me that I was never going to bear a second child. We both tried very hard not to spoil Sarah, and not have her tagged as a "lonely only" child, but also how could we not give her what she deserved or needed? I convinced myself that we were not spoiling her. There are no rule books for motherhood or being a parent and it is simply a bit of trial and error; mostly common sense, how your parents were with you and the passage of time, which brings experience. We all just hope that we do a decent job of it, but only time can really tell.

Over the coming year, we were so wrapped up and busy with Sarah Jane and the house that we didn't really go on holiday. However, we did manage to go away for our first weekend since having her; we went with friends Debbie & Kevin to Chester. Paul's mum had kindly offered to have her for us, so we booked it and arranged to go by train as none of us had a car at the time.

I was so excited; we all were, chatting all the way. Chester was only about hour and a half by train from where we lived and we had planned the weekend to make the most of it. As the train slowed near our final stop, we prepared to leave the carriage with our luggage in hand and moved towards the door when the guard appeared and, looking rather confused, asked us where were going. Chester, we replied. "Not on this train you're not. I'm afraid this is the London train and we won't stop now till we arrive in Euston!" I'm not sure which was worse: the feelings of stupidity, embarrassment or disappointment, or at missing half a day of our short weekend sitting on a train, and now without a seat as they had promptly been acquired by other grateful passengers.

The guard was most sympathetic and helpful. He led us to the guard's van and offered to buy us all a sandwich; we hadn't taken any food as we had planned to have breakfast in Chester. We couldn't have been more grateful to him. Eventually we did arrive in Chester and our nice hotel and we did have a lovely time. We all saw the funny side of it and made us laugh throughout the entire weekend – or at least what was left of it.

Other than Chester, Paul and I hadn't been anywhere since we'd married and certainly not abroad. We did have lovely little breaks in Barnstaple, in North Devon, with Paul's parents when they visited his grandparents or his aunt and uncle in Ilfracombe, all of whom we were very fond. We also spent holidays and weekends with my sister, Diane and her husband, Alan and son, Mark at their home in Penrith in the North lakes, a most beautiful place.

Diane married the year after me on the first Saturday in October 1982 to Alan, a lovely man whom she met at work in NORWEB. I love them dearly. He has been a

true and loyal friend and he is so kind, as is my sister. Generous, caring and sincere, but above all he has been like a brother, a real brother (unlike the eldest one of the two I had).

Diane and Alan had recently bought a timeshare in Scotland in 1986 and kindly invited us to go along with them and we gratefully accepted, of course. Paul had passed his driving test first time and after just six lessons only weeks before, and we had bought our first car in Penrith whilst there for the weekend. It was a lovely metallic cobalt blue Renault with low mileage. She was a bargain we simply couldn't refuse. So on the week with Diane and Alan he drove us to Ballater, through rather treacherous conditions at times, especially over Glenshee, but he managed very well indeed especially as this was his first lengthy journey.

We arrived at Craigendarroch, all in one piece, at two o'clock having set off at ten o'clock, with two stops en-route. Sarah had been as good as gold in her new car seat in the back, whether singing, eating or sleeping her way through the journey (fortunately plenty of the latter). We checked in, collected the key and headed for the lodge. We opened the door, entered a lovely hallway, and began to explore it all. I was astounded, we both were, at the pure luxury throughout; it had two bedrooms and a pull down bed in the lounge, so could sleep up to six people; it was an open-plan kitchen-diner, leading onto a balcony with a wonderful view. The hotel on site had leisure facilities, including a dry ski slope, all for our use during the duration, and a cosy bar, restaurant, a crèche and a beauty salon.

This was going to be a holiday of a different kind and I knew we were going to love it there. We unpacked and headed for the indoor pool, where we spent a great deal of our time, either first thing in the morning or just before our evening meal. Sarah was a real water baby, which was something I had encouraged from birth by taking her to the weekly mother and toddler sessions in the local baths. She was very happy and content in the water, loved it in fact. Getting her out was the problem.

We went walking and sightseeing during the day, finding new walks and places to see, including Glen Muick, carefully looking out for all the red deer in the hills and Braemar, where the famous annual highland games are held. Aberdeen (the granite city) is not too far away either, a most interesting place to visit with many attractions including Castles, museums, art galleries and great for shopping.

Closer to the complex is Aboyne, a pretty little place surrounded by the most stunning scenery for miles around; snow-covered mountains scenes that I had only ever seen on postcards or pictures, some of which literally took my breath away.

We were coming sadly to the end of our week of adventure, during which Paul and I talked and enquired about buying a week there ourselves. I was a little surprised at his impulse, not to mention the cost, and was at first rather cautious. On the last morning, we went to view a slightly smaller lodge on the complex a short distance away. It was lovely, a rather different layout, with similar fixtures and fittings throughout, perhaps more contemporary in style but on a smaller scale, with this one having one twin bedroom and the pull down double bed so would sleep four people. We were very impressed, so much so that by five o'clock that afternoon we had agreed to buy a week.

An additional benefit with the timeshare agreement was that we could join a consortium that would allow us to bank and exchange our week with various other places abroad. This very much appealed to me; you simply paid an exchange fee and the cost of the flights because the accommodation was already paid for within the system. I now could see the world opening up before my very eyes, a world I was so keen to see and explore and this seemed like an easy option in which to do just that. Whatever we chose to do, I knew we had a holiday every year for the rest of our lives in beautiful Scotland, come what may. I was so excited and thrilled that we had been invited.

# CHAPTER SEVENTEEN

In the late '80s we made two rather disastrous house moves: one to a lovely new detached bungalow in Swarthmoor, once again initiated by Paul whilst we were away for the weekend at my sisters. He had found the bungalow on a new estate in Swarthmoor (the place where his grandparents once lived) near Ulverston and I felt rather browbeaten into viewing it, if I am honest, but we viewed it the next week and ended up buying it. It turned out to be too inconvenient for me with regards to transport, as I don't drive, and the estate was rather quiet and predominantly seemed to attract the 'older generation'. Therefore, after less than a year, Paul disappointedly and somewhat reluctantly said we were to move back to the island. (He did eventually agree that, in hindsight, we were too young to live in a bungalow and that they were for retirement years.

We then made a hasty move to a really quite awful, poky semi-detached house. It was in an enviable position, overlooking the sea from the back and being literally a hop, skip and a jump from the back gate to the shore. Another positive was being surrounded by a street full of the friendliest neighbours, all of whom were more or less our age. The camaraderie was wonderful and, although I never liked the house at all, its location and our neighbours helped make up for all that it lacked in character and charm.

By this time, about 1994, Paul was working in the drawing offices at VSEL, which he really seemed to enjoy, having chosen a different career path a few years previously. I always tried to encourage him to progress and move on, trying not to be too pushy, as he did tend to lack either self-confidence or enthusiasm at times, but then so can we all. I knew he was capable of doing more and his move to the drawing offices had proved my point and had been a very successful transition indeed, for his career and salary.

VSEL had announced even more redundancies. The end of the Cold War in 1991 had marked a reduction in demand for military ships and the workforce was dropping fast, plummeting from 14,500 to only 5,800. This was causing great unrest in the town and whilst we had managed to escape the previous rounds of "Dear John's," as they had come to be known, we were becoming concerned about the safety and security of his job, although Paul was trying to protect me from worrying unnecessarily and remained calm. I had been thinking long and hard for a while now about the possibilities. What we would do if the worst were to happen? It scared me.

He came home from work one particular evening and we sat after our meal and talked; I asked him about the possibilities of moving to a "safer" department or trying to transfer to another site, or maybe even a possible re-location package somewhere. Understandably, he was very wary, in particular because of the "disaster move," as he called it, to Swarthmoor. "If you can't live 8 miles away, how on earth can you think of moving further afield?" and yes, his concerns were justified. However, I put my case and thoughts to him and that this was a completely different and potentially more serious situation. This was his job and our livelihood so I would be more than happy to consider a move to a different place, should it be viable.

I had been thinking positively about the situation and was becoming very excited about the whole prospect. I was also thinking that maybe it was time for a complete change for us, but also that we should take the initiative and act before our hand was forced.

I didn't want to push him too hard as I knew his boundaries and after all it was he who would have to take a new job, should he be fortunate enough to find something suitable. We talked at length about it over the weekend and he was starting to come round to the idea, or perhaps I had convinced him that I was ready to move to wherever the job would take us. I also felt that I needed to do something to make right the last two failed house moves. It was a bit of a gamble for sure, but I somehow knew I could do this. I just had to for us him and our future.

Over the coming week he had spent time meticulously writing up his CV and decided to send it to a number of relevant and recommended recruitment agencies. We waited and hoped for the best whilst trying to remain positive.

The following week on Tuesday evening, he had gone to the local leisure centre for a swim. I was home preparing dinner when the phone rang; I answered and a most polite and well-spoken man introduced himself and asked to speak to Paul. I explained that he wasn't at home and asked if I could take a message and ask him to call him back when he returned home. Once again, he gave me his name and said where he was from and it was I then that I recognised it as one of the recruitment agencies to whom Paul had sent his CV. The man explained that he needed to speak with him as soon as was possible; he gave his number, thanked me for taking the message and hung up.

I was so excited that I immediately rang the sports centre and said to the young man that answered that I urgently needed to speak to Paul Barker and could he please call him from the pool. Immediately, I heard him call for Paul and he instantly came to the phone. I relayed the message and he rushed home straight away to ring the recruitment agency back. After finishing the call, he excitedly explained the reason and outcome of the call. He had been invited to a job interview in Dorchester, which he had accepted. He had no idea where Dorchester was; the only Dorchester we knew of was the posh hotel in London! We took the map from the study to see just where it was and get his bearings finding that it was approximately 340 miles away in the south of the country.

The next day, having spoken to his manager, he booked his train and packed his case, leaving on Thursday ready for his interview on Friday morning. He arrived after quite an arduous journey to rather basic accommodation above a local Dorchester pub called the White Hart. He was not terribly impressed with the place at all but resigned himself to the overnight stay there. He decided to have a bit of a walk and a brief look at the town before it got too late, as night was beginning to fall. His first impressions of the market town were very positive he really liked what he saw.

# CHAPTER EIGHTEEN

He felt that the interviews had gone rather well and was told he should hear within a week as they had further people to interview. He immediately liked the senior man that interviewed him and felt very at ease. So, after a two-hour interview, he set off to head back home. When he arrived home, he was very positive; he had had time to reflect on it and was feeling quietly hopeful. Tuesday morning's post arrived and amongst it was a letter addressed to him, so I called him to tell him, as I could see from the postmark it was regarding the interview. I wanted to, but I didn't open it.

At 5.30 he came home and slowly opened the letter and there it was: a job offer and he couldn't really believe it. I was so pleased for him and for us all; the days that followed were busy with him finalising the re-location package, salary and all the terms and conditions. We were so happy and I felt above all a great sense of pride in him. This was a very special occasion; drinking during the week was something he neither agreed with nor encouraged, but I went to the fridge and opened a bottle of wine to toast our new life.

We both had much to think about, consider and plan, not least how and when to tell everyone, as up to that point we had said nothing to anyone. We decided to tell our parents that coming weekend; it all had happened so fast and we needed a day or two to get our heads around it and put plans and in place for all that lay ahead. Although Paul was re-locating within the company, he still needed to serve his notice period there. Then we needed to arrange valuations for the house to give us an idea as to what we could afford in Dorchester so we could begin looking online at suitable properties. We also looked at solicitors, schools for Sarah Jane, read up on the area and locality, looked for removal companies that would travel the distance involved … the list was exhaustive but we tried to cover everything we could possibly imagine.

Saturday morning arrived and the time had come to spread our news; something neither of us was looking forward to doing at all. Whilst we were both terribly excited about everything, we knew that the feeling would not be reciprocated.

We called at my parents first and Dad opened the door, his face beaming, talking in his daft Donald Duck voice and clearly in a great mood (as usual, although he had been prone to mood swings since having a minor stroke a few years before). Oh dear, I thought, this was going to wipe that smile from his cheeky face and I suddenly began to feel guilty and rather nervous. Mum was in the kitchen, standing at the sink, already filling up the kettle as she had seen us coming through the window.

I started to help, getting the cups from the cupboard, whilst looking over at Mum as she cut the cake she had made to have with the tea. We all went in the lounge and I prepared to tell them. Sarah was sitting on Mum's knee already, chomping on the chocolate bar her Nana had given her. She was always stocked up with goodies for her; Paul used to get quite cross at times, complaining that she would ruin her teeth, or not eat her meal, but that's what grannies do.

# CHAPTER NINETEEN

I took a deep breath and began: "We have some exciting news for you," I began with a smile, "and, no, I am not pregnant!" They both knew by now that was never going to happen, I had talked endlessly to her about it over the years and by now she had resigned herself to the obvious.

"Paul has been offered a wonderful job opportunity and, given the latest round of more redundancies in the yard and with all that uncertainty and worry we can't just keep praying and hoping he will be safe time and again. So he decided to look around and see what else was available in his line of work." I continued. "He sent off his CV to a few agencies and was invited for an interview last Friday and got the job offer this week. After discussing it together he's accepted." Phew, that was it! I had done it and was shaking.

I sat back in my seat looked over at them on the sofa, both of them now wearing a rather shocked and disappointed expression. They didn't say anything for a moment then Mum broke the silence.

"Where is it?" she asked, voice slightly raised.

"Dorchester," Paul replied.

"Where's that?"

"On the south coast, Mum," I replied. Mum and Dad stared at each other, seeming not to understand; it clearly didn't register so she asked again, so I repeated myself. Oh dear. I sensed what was coming and although Mum did try to be upbeat, I could tell she was in a state of shock. My Dad was a very sensitive man who could never hide his feelings; he was quite clearly devastated and began to cry.

I wasn't quite prepared for this outburst, but I had to remain strong, so I attempted to console them both, as Mum by then also had tears in her eyes. I agreed that it was unexpected for them and would take time for them to adjust, but pleaded that they try to think positively about it; they should be proud that he had done something to avoid the possible threat of redundancy at some point.

At that time, they didn't see it like that and as far as they were concerned he had a job and might not get finished. They were very much of the opinion that we should wait and see if it happened and then do something about it if it did.

"I'm afraid we cannot live like that, Mum," Paul explained. "It's too stressful wondering and looking over your shoulder all the time to see if he comes in with a white envelope and then if he did I'd have to find a job along with all the other poor folk that will have received the same news." No, that was not the thing to do for either of us. We stayed a while longer trying to convince and console my bereft parents, worrying that we then had to go to his parents and do it all again. Somehow, I felt they both would be more positive and understanding.

How wrong I was. We arrived just as Dad had come in for something for one of his projects he was constructing in the shed, which was where he generally immersed himself in whatever he was doing. Sarah went into the conservatory to read her book and the rest of us sat down while Paul explained it all again from the beginning. There was a deathly silence and Dad stood up saying, "You're not really serious are you? This is a joke isn't it?"

"No, Dad, it isn't," I replied. "We are doing this because we have to and more importantly we want to. It's very exciting for us.

"I know things are going to be very different but there are so many positives if you think about it. We really would appreciate some positive support here, this has been a big decision for us and we are both feeling very positive about it all." His mum was speechless. This was so hard and I couldn't believe the reactions from all of them. Of course, we knew it wouldn't be easy and Paul and I had both had time to get used to the idea and were now just excited about the prospect. It was just sad that none of them could be supportive; we were so disappointed.

We set off back home after quite a long period of heavy discussions to hear the phone ringing; it was my Mum to say that Doug (Paul's Dad) had rung her to ask what they made of this fiasco. I was not happy at all, and neither was Paul. However cross I was feeling I decided we had to allow them time to get used to the idea, as it must have been a huge shock for them in fairness. We decided to just leave them all to gather their thoughts and in a few days' time they might begin to think differently. I hoped and prayed that they would become more positive about it.

On Thursday morning, my parents came round to visit; I didn't work Thursdays so they took a chance I would be home. I was in the garden at the time pegging out my washing and they just walked in as was normal (strangely quite a Northern thing I understand) when I heard them calling me. Suddenly they appeared at the door, Mum looking very upset and Dad not looking much happier either. Oh dear, this was not going to be pleasant. I had been brought up to speak when you're spoken to and not to answer back your elders, although on occasion my patience was tried and I somehow sensed that this was possibly going to be just one of those.

I went inside and immediately put the kettle on, another typically friendly, Northern thing to do. I carried the tea to the lounge and they were both sat on the settee, Dad quite stony faced, when Mum suddenly turned to me: "Susan," (another sign she was annoyed or upset, as she never called me Susan as a rule), "are you happy?"

"What?" I replied, "Why do you ask that? Of course I am happy, very happy."

"You have changed since you married," and she added, "why? What is it? Is he forcing you to do this? Moving *all* the way down south? *You* wouldn't do this! *You* wouldn't leave us all alone here."

George was in London, where he'd moved to run a pub with his gay partner. However, Diane was living in the lakes and not too far away and Phillip of course happily married with three lovely children, all lived nearby. They weren't being left "all alone."

"Now you are threatening to go away and desert us," Mum continued. "We will never see you anymore; it's too far away for us to pop in for a cup of tea. I can't possibly drive all that way to come and see you either, and the train fare is much too expensive – I know as I have enquired already. We will only see you when you come back here to visit, and you will be too busy living your own life and working there." Mum and Dad were both crying and I was fighting back the tears – I couldn't possibly let them see they had got to me.

I was reeling. I just couldn't believe what I was hearing; it was nothing but blackmail! How could they? How dare they be so selfish and inconsiderate? I appreciated that they were finding it hard but this was outrageous. My heart was pounding in my chest, my ears were ringing and I felt tears stinging my eyes but I was trying so very hard to appear calm and collected.

I turned to my mother and calmly said, "That really is quite unfair and most unkind. I will not have you come into my home and try to make me feel guilty about trying to do something positive with our lives, for trying to secure a safe future for our family. I find it quite ironic for you to be like this with me when you have a son in London who has been unquestionably the bane of my life, whom over the years has tortured and tormented me, most of which you were made totally aware of, but lots of which you know nothing about.

"You never tried to protect me or even seriously consider what exactly he did to me. You didn't want to know; it was easier for you to turn a blind eye without even considering the consequences. I think you sometimes thought I was making it up, but I can tell you without any doubt that I wasn't. He is an evil, sadistic person, and I hate him for all he has done."

They were both sat together, still and quiet with their tea and my Dad's favourite, Eccles cakes, virtually untouched on his plate staring at me. I started to feel uneasy and rather guilty, but my upbringing to remain silent and not be cheeky to your elders was no more. I knew that everything every single word I'd said was true and well overdue.

I stood and went into the kitchen, shaking like a leaf and feeling more than a little awkward, but I just had to say it. If there is one thing in life I have learnt about myself it is not to let things simmer away; I have to deal with problems or worries straight away before things become harder to deal with. Part of this I blame on George making me promise not to tell Mum, Dad or anyone when he had been cruel and brutal, threatening that he would make it even worse for me the next time we were alone. I couldn't bear the thought of even more torture, for I really never knew his boundaries at all and daren't push the boundaries.

Mum came into the kitchen; I was washing my teacup and had set it down on the draining board when she approached me and put her arm on my shoulder. She could see my eyes were red and that I was very upset, aware that she too had over-stepped the mark this time. Paul often used to say he could sense when my parents had been round for one reason or another, usually because I was wound up, feeling unable to answer back. He was right, but I had certainly answered back this time, that's for sure.

She apologised, after a fashion, and then went on to say it was only because they were going to miss us all. But again she said they had been concerned about Paul's apparent 'power' over me and they were becoming quite worried about it. They liked him, I know they did, and often said as much; but there was always something I couldn't quite put my finger on and now the light was dawning. I assured them as best I could that I was happy, that he was a good husband and a very good father and I saw no reason for them to be concerned.

I had to admit he was the boss in many ways, especially when it came to money matters. He was the one to hold the purse strings but that never bothered me at all and I was quite happy with our arrangement. He always said that I was the one that wore the trousers, and I maybe tried to convince myself of that, but I was happy and we had been married now for twelve years and were about to embark on a new life. Despite what they were saying or thinking, I was fully behind this move and, in fact, to a large degree I was the one at the helm. The disaster move (Paul's words) to Swarthmoor was always in the back of his mind, I know it was, and I fully understood why; but everything about this move just felt so 'right'.

# CHAPTER TWENTY

They both left and the atmosphere was very sombre. I waved her little brown Ford Fiesta out of sight, returned to the lounge and looked again at my dad's untouched Eccles cake on the plate and began to cry. My head was spinning and I was very angry, but moreover I was so disappointed.

I wasn't sure what I was most upset about: was it their selfishness at our imminent move to the south to what we hoped to be a wonderful new life, or was it because of their obvious concerns about my marriage? This really was a shock. One thing I did know was that Paul would be aware of their visit. How do I tell him, "Oh my parents are worried about me. They think you're a control freak and you don't make me happy"? Whatever I said, he definitely wasn't going to like it any more than me, but I had to tell him.

I was feeling so let down by them; I had hoped for some moral support and understanding, and maybe even just a tad of encouragement for having the foresight to do something positive and show initiative. However, I'd received nothing of the kind from either of them.

It had totally ruined my day; I had planned to achieve so much as there were still lots to be done with packing and letter writing, finding doctors, dentists and the like. We did receive confirmation that day saying that we had secured a place for Sarah Jane at St Osmund's school, which was wonderful news. The headmaster, Mr Davies, asked that we take her in so we could all meet him and have a look around the school on our next visit, which was to be next week, so that was something else to tick off the 'to do' list. At least something positive had happened that day.

I decided that I needed to get out of the house as I now had the headache from hell and knew I could do nothing more until I'd got rid of it. I went to the cupboard, donned my black wool military coat, pulled on my knee-high boots and threw my cream, fluffy scarf around my neck. Even though there was no wind and a fair bit of blue in the sky, it was a very cool March morning. I set off out the back gate and across to the beach, up to Biggar Bank right along the shoreline then up onto the path, encouraged to do so by the waves as the tide was coming in quite fast. I was trying so hard to clear my head of the stinging, selfish words from Mum.

I had reached Biggar village, stopping to feed grass to the two horses that came inquisitively to the fence to say hello. One was piebald, the other skewbald, both well kempt and fine looking horses. I then turned back and headed along the shoreline once again.

I stopped for a cheeky and childish sit on the swings in the little play area along the way and couldn't help but notice a few odd glances from dog walkers and passers-by, but I didn't care. One little girl with her granny seemed to find it quite amusing she and kept looking over her shoulder at me with a lovely smile. I returned her smile when the girl ran over to sit on the swing next to me and continued to watch me with fascination. She began talking to me in her sweet little voice, asking what I was doing.

"You look funny on a swing – you're a lady" and she laughed loudly. "What's your name?" Her granny, who was sitting close by on the recently-erected bench in memory of some poor soul, heard her and scolded her for being cheeky and nosey.

I said I didn't mind at all, told her my name and learnt her name was Maisie; she was four and a chatty little maid too. She was also very adorable, looking so sweet in her red fluffy coat and black wellingtons. She also wore a white fur hat with a huge pompom on the top, all finished off with matching mittens, which I noticed were mucky and mud-stained from playing.

She talked confidently with me we then both walked over to play on the roundabout together, at her insistence of course as Granny couldn't manage to push her on it, let alone want to join her play. I always loved the roundabout as a child; my favourite was the banana slide but there wasn't one here, just three swings and a little see-saw all thickly painted dark green to weather the elements of the sea.

I suddenly noticed now that my headache had completely disappeared; we were laughing and having a lovely time together. What a chatterbox she was and I had learnt by now so much about her: that her favourite toy was her cuddly dog called 'Ruffles' who was now at home sleeping in his basket on her bedroom floor; her favourite book was The Owl and the Pussy cat and number one cartoon was Postman Pat. We then concluded somehow that she had a severe dislike of carrots.

She was such a dear little character. I was thinking how similar to how Sarah Jane had been at that age in some of her ways; she also loved this little play area when she was younger. It did take me back to when we used to visit the playground but, at almost nine years old, she was insistent that she was far too big for such things. I don't believe we ever grow out of it. In fact, I was on the swings in a park in Scotland recently and I secretly loved it but shhh, don't tell anyone.

Granny came over to thank me for taking the time with Maisie and we got chatting. They were from Newcastle and visiting on holiday for a few days, staying with her son (Maisie's Dad). He had been made compulsorily redundant from the yard five months ago and had quite understandably not taken it well at all. He was just a few years older than Paul and me. I chose not to tell her of our situation; partly because I was feeling much better and certainly didn't want to get upset again, but neither did I want to feel I was rubbing salt in their wound. It must have been terribly sad for them, as it was for many people at that time.

It was affecting so many families in so many ways. However, without wanting to sound selfish, I couldn't help but feel more sure than ever that what we were about to do was absolutely and undoubtedly the right thing. I dreaded the thought of us being forced into dealing with a redundancy; it must be so demeaning.

We then said our goodbyes and I wished them all well and hoped her son would find something very soon. Maisie came to hug me then and said, donning a huge smile "Thank you for playing with me. Mummy won't ever come on the swings or roundabout with me and I can't wait to tell her you did it." And with that they left,

144

Maisie waving enthusiastically as she walked away, chattering to Granny fifty to the dozen. I could only imagine what she was saying.

I set off back home again after skimming a few stones in the sea, or at least trying to as I never have been able to master the knack of skimming stone, even selecting the right pebble to do so, but I gave it a fair shot. It must have been lunchtime as my belly was banging, and when I looked at my watch, I couldn't believe it was quarter to three. I had been out for almost three hours, but aside from being hungry, I was now feeling so much better.

Back home I had a very light lunch as it was so late, then I completed a few jobs from the 'to do' list as I was feeling more myself again. I then decided to have a lovely long soak in the bath before preparing tea, as I was now feeling rather chilly. I added my favourite Sanctuary bath oil and immersed myself, laying quietly thinking about my day and what our future may hold.

I am a woman of quite simple means really, I thought to myself; all I ask is for us to be happy, living in a nice house, nothing too grand and expensive, and nothing that would require us living above our means at all. I am by no means a risk taker when it comes to financial affairs but then the money was always down to Paul. Nor am I pushy or demanding. I just want to be happy and feel loved, and I was.

Suddenly I felt I was trying to justify myself and I didn't need to do this and what's more, I shouldn't have to. I guess the atmosphere of this morning was still lurking in the background but I was determined not to let it get to me again and spoil my mood, so I pulled myself from my reverie and decided to put on some music and dance. There is nothing like a good tune with a great drumbeat to sing along to 'Go your own way' from Fleetwood Mac's *Rumours* album was swiftly chosen and the volume turned up high. Oh, I suddenly felt so much better. Sarah was being collected from school and taken to Grandma's for tea and they would bring her home at seven o'clock. That meant it was just the two of us and I decided I would make a lasagne, which was nice and easy and a favourite. Paul got home around five-thirty and as soon as he came in the door, he guessed (as I knew he would) that my parents had been; it was almost as though it was painted on the walls.

I began telling him exactly what had been said and, as expected, he didn't appreciate it, not one little bit. First, he didn't like that I had once again been upset by them, but he was even more disappointed they had felt that I wasn't happy. He pressed me for reassurance and I told him that I was very happy. After talking a little more about it, we decided to say no more on the matter and retain our positive approach. Quite honestly, by then we were just counting the days until we went, wishing it would now be sooner rather than later.

# CHAPTER TWENTY-ONE

I was very fond of both my in-laws, especially Mum or
Ma as I referred to her. She really was a wonderful
mother–in-law in fact they really don't come any better.
We both got on exceptionally well; she never liked
calling me her 'daughter-in-law', especially when
introducing me to anyone new as she felt it somewhat
derogatory. She always regarded me as her daughter and
to me that was most acceptable indeed. I often thought I
was very lucky to have her; I love her to this day and
nothing will ever change that. She has always been a
wonderful Grandma to Sarah-Jane, spending a large
amount of time with her, either on her own or with us all
together. Whether Dad was there depended on his shift
or his latest project or collecting obsession (of which he
had many), but Grandma was always there for her grand-
daughter.

We would go for walks in and around the Lakes,
which wasn't too far at all, sometimes making a day of it
by taking a picnic, or sometimes simply staying in the
caravan they had bought in Cockermouth. Often she
would just have Sarah-Jane to herself, maybe picking her
up from school to take her back to play and have tea or
perhaps to have a baking session. Sometimes at
weekends she wanted her to stay overnight for company;
she'd bought her a lovely cot when she was new born

then swapped it for a single bed when she was older and had outgrown the cot. It was a lovely 'nursery' that she had created. Obviously this was an additional benefit for Paul and me as we could go out if we wanted without babysitting worries; we were very lucky as that was something we never really had to think about. Mum was really going to miss us all, but Sarah in particular, and Sarah was going to miss her, too, and that was going to be probably the hardest part, for them especially.

In the following weeks, once our family had all seen that we had put the house on the market, with the 'FOR SALE' sign in the front garden, they all began to understand; I avoid the word 'accept' here because I knew deep down they never would, most certainly not my parents, but in particular my father.

Paul moved down alone to start his new job and lived in a B&B through the week Monday to Friday and we would take it in turns travelling each weekend. One weekend Sarah and I would come down on the train; Paul would meet us at Bristol Temple Meads and we would stay in a hotel for the weekend. The next weekend he would come home Friday and leave after Sunday lunch to drive down. Sometimes he would stay Sunday evening and we would go to bed early so he could get a reasonable night before leaving around four o'clock on Monday morning; it wasn't ideal but it did allow us to spend a little more time together.

Over the course of the weekends, Sarah and I had been going to Dorchester I fell in love with the place. This lovely little market town of around 20,000 people sits on the banks of the River Frome, in the Frome valley, just south of the Dorset Downs. Its roots date back to prehistoric times, with early settlements around

Maiden Castle. Nearby it boasts the home of the novelist Thomas Hardy, whose novel The Mayor of Casterbridge was based in the town.

Whilst in Dorchester we were busy trawling around the estate agents to see what properties were available and fortunately, we found the one! Paul had heard about a new estate and suggested we look around during our next visit. When we went, we found a lovely newly-built house. It was ideal; three bedrooms, detached, with a nice-sized garden and garage (something we had never had before). It also overlooked the school playing fields so had a lovely, open private aspect from the front elevation.

I was so excited, but we still had to sell ours first and it had just been registered for sale with our agent; therefore, I had to exercise a little patience, and that is not something I was terribly good at. We went out for dinner that evening and talked at length about the house and the area and we both loved it all; even Sarah liked it and we both felt she needed to feel safe and happy, too.

We had had a lovely weekend but it was over far too quickly and before I knew it, we were on the train heading home again, with no one to greet us when we arrived. That was strange for me and something to which I was still adjusting. After all, I was part instigator for the situation. However, on this occasion it was not the best of journeys as there were important line works being undertaken which meant the last leg of our journey from Lancaster to Barrow was in a taxi, all courtesy of the train company, of course, but it added over an hour to our journey. We didn't get home till after ten that night; we'd been up early as we had to vacate our room by eleven o'clock, having eaten an amazing breakfast cooked by Stuart. He was the owner of the Casterbridge Hotel and was always so understanding and appreciative of our situation; we had grown very fond of him over the recent months having got to know him quite well.

It had been a long day. I had a very well behaved but very tired daughter with me; we got through the front door and I just left the case in the hallway. Sarah went to brush her teeth and wash her face and then I tucked her into bed with a kiss and cuddle as usual before making myself a cup of tea to take up to bed. I really disliked coming back to an empty house and tonight seemed even worse as it was so much later than usual. I went upstairs and washed, as it was too late for baths or showers.

All I was ready for was sleep and so I climbed once again into a half empty bed. I missed Paul so much and would often sleep on his side of the bed to help me feel closer to him; I always whispered him goodnight. Thankfully, I had been very organised and had prepared for school and work before we'd left on Friday so all I had to do now was drink my tea and sleep.

Waking up before the alarm at seven o'clock, my tea untouched from last night, I dragged myself from my cosy, warm bed to start the day and a fresh new week.

The week passed rather quickly as I was busy at work as well as planning and preparing for the future. On the Friday, I opened the post to find a letter from our estate agent stating we had received an offer on our house. I hadn't even known that anyone had been in, so this had come as a great surprise; as I read on, I found that we'd been offered the asking price. I was ecstatic. Paul was coming home that evening and I couldn't wait to see him, even more so now that I had this great news to share. What a difference a week makes.

When he walked in, I was in the kitchen adding the final ingredients of button mushrooms to braising steak, one of his favourite meals. I had prepared the potatoes and vegetables (peas and carrots, the only veg he would eat, despite my years of coaxing, although he did eat so much fruit every day so I didn't worry too much about it). I put the pot back in the oven to finish off and I turned to see him beaming at me, so pleased to see me and to be home again. We briefly kissed and hugged each other; he wasn't the most demonstrative person, but I knew he loved me very much and missed me during our time apart. He then stepped back, looked at me smiling and asked me "What is it, Sue?" He knew me very well and I simply couldn't contain myself any longer.

I had planned just to give him the letter amongst his little pile of post that had gathered since we last saw each other. He always loved to open his post and it was always one of the first things he did when he came through the door. But I simply couldn't wait any longer and blurted it out.

"We have had an offer on the house! And it's for the asking price! And they're cash buyers!" I grinned and passed him the letter. He asked if it was really true and told him to open the letter and see. "I think you would agree that this calls for a celebration," I said as he read the letter and I took the wine I'd bought earlier out of the fridge.

It was Friday and he was home so it was allowed. He read the letter again then looked across the table at me eagerly, reached for the wine and poured two glasses. He handed me my glass, raised his and toasted, "Cheers to us and our new life in Dorchester!" He then leaned forward to kiss me.

"Everything is all falling into place," I said. "We can put in an offer on the house in Dorchester now," hoping that it was still available of course. "Let's call the estate agent in the morning and speak to them and see where we go from there." We couldn't believe it − my goodness I was so happy.

Saturday morning we were awake early, still buzzing with excitement about the offer but anxious at the same time about the house in Dorchester. We decided that I would call the agents at 9 a.m., and see what the situation was with the house. We had decided to wait and see what the outcome was before telling Sarah, as we didn't want to unsettle her if anything were different. We got up, had breakfast then whilst Paul was in the shower I called them. I explained the situation and said we would like to put in an offer. The lady took all the details and said she would need to call me back as needed to remind herself of details having been on holiday most of the week. I waited patiently for the call, my tummy tying itself knots and fifteen minutes later, she rang.

"Well I have both good and not so good news for you: the house is still available, as far as I can see, but there is no one around today to speak to about submitting your offer. Someone else viewed it on Friday afternoon who was also very interested but it would be Monday before we can speak to the sales office. I can get someone to call you Monday morning to discuss it further then if you'd like?" I agreed, but was disappointed. There was nothing else I could do but hope and wait for the call.

I updated Paul when he came into the kitchen and we just promised to remain positive and wait for the call. We had a lovely weekend, just mooching around locally; he did so much travelling with work that he understandably didn't like to go too far on his weekends at home and there were a few jobs that needed to be done in the house.

Sunday came round so quickly and he set off back after a late lunch. He couldn't stay the night as he had a big meeting in Camberley the next morning and it was to be an early start. I always shed a tear as he drove out of sight. It was hard for us all but necessary to achieve our aim and hopefully wasn't to be too much longer.

Fortunately, I had Sarah with me; she was lovely company, which helped a great deal. In fact, I felt this time together had brought the two of us closer together as she was very much a Dad's girl, perhaps as most girls are. I've always wondered whether my delayed introduction to her after her birth had had a bearing on that, but at least Paul had been there to hold and care for her and that was the most important thing. However, with Paul away so much our bond was growing and I really appreciated my time with her; she was a good girl, a great friend and a wonderful daughter.

# CHAPTER TWENTY-TWO

I was feeling hopeful that there was light at the end of the tunnel, pending tomorrow's call (fingers and everything crossed) and it wasn't going to be too long to wait and find out.

I was up early, started preparing myself for work and made sure that Sarah was all ready and dressed for school before having breakfast together. Our neighbour's daughter Janine had come to call for Sarah. They had started to walk in together and they'd both pressured us to let them do it. Janine's mum, Chris, used to follow them in the car (without them knowing) just to be sure they were safe and being sensible. The school was only a ten-minute walk for them so I watched them from the bedroom window until they were out of sight.

I could hear them chattering away fifty to the dozen all the way down the street. They had become good friends to each other, Sarah almost nine and Janine almost eight. They were both very competent and capable otherwise we wouldn't have let them do it. All these things were on my mind with regards to the imminent move and I did worry very much about how much the disruption would affect Sarah. I couldn't help but hope it would be better for her in the long run: a better schooling system, a lovely new house in a beautiful part of the world. If we didn't try it we would never know and if it didn't work out we could come back again perhaps, something I hoped was not going to be necessary. I was putting my heart and soul into the move and thinking positively as I really wanted this to work for us all.

I finished getting ready for work after clearing up then I rang the sales office in Dorchester, my fingers crossed as I typed the number into the phone. I smiled at myself for doing it but I just thought it might help. A lady answered instantly and I recognised her voice; she was the agent who gave us the key to view the property the previous weekend. I began to tell her our latest developments to find that she already knew as the girl from Saturday had passed on the information via email. She went on to explain that as far as she was aware the house was still available and that the other people interested had not yet put their house on the market so were not in such a good position as we were.

I was told that she needed to call her director to pass on our offer and situation, after which she promised she would get back to me after three o'clock that afternoon, once I had returned from work and hopefully with an answer. What a long six hours that was! Sure enough, the call came at twelve minutes past three precisely – I was sat by the phone waiting – and it was positive! I simply couldn't believe it! They'd accepted the offer as, although it had been slightly under the asking price, as they knew it would sell, we were in such a strong position as our buyers were cash buyers and desperately wanted to be in within six weeks. I was smiling from ear to ear on the phone and she really seemed genuinely pleased for us; I liked her when I'd met her the previous week and thought then that she had a nice manner about her and seemed most sincere.

I had to ring Paul with the news, as I couldn't wait until he called me that evening; he called every day between seven and eight, depending on his whereabouts. It was never a long call, just a quick chat to catch-up before speaking to Sarah to say goodnight. Unfortunately, I couldn't get hold of him so I had to leave it until the evening.

Just after seven o'clock, he called having returned from Camberley after a long day and heavy meetings. I tried to remain calm but ended up blurting it out almost immediately with excitement.

"We have got the house! The offer was accepted!" at which point I shrieked excitedly, before going on to fill him in on every little detail, whether he wanted to hear it all or not, after which I drew breath and laughed. His ears must have been stinging.

"Blimey, well done you!" he replied. "I best come home again this weekend then – there's a lot to do."

He's never really displayed any great emotion about things, unlike me: I am most excitable and certainly not backwards in coming forwards; sometimes to the extreme, I know, but that's me. I think I carried the excitement for the two of us sometimes, although I could definitely tell that he was very pleased. It was all systems go from here on in and I just couldn't wait. It was really happening now and it felt marvellous.

However, it didn't all go completely smoothly. Our buyer threatened to pull out over the moving date. We didn't have any power over that as it was down to the solicitors doing all the checks and paperwork, but it all was eventually sorted quite quickly and a moving date was agreed. It was to be the first bank holiday weekend in May and we had already reached the end of March.

The day eventually arrived and we were up and organised very early. My friend Chris from across the road came over to say her goodbyes, but sadly broke down in tears as soon as I opened the front door. She apologised between the sobs, saying she really didn't want us to go, that she was going to miss me terribly and finally that she couldn't bare it any longer before running home heartbroken.

We had become great friends and the camaraderie in the street was still as good as it ever had been. I would miss them all and Chris in particular. She was very special and I had become very fond of her during the four years we had lived there. We promised to stay in touch and said that we would see her when we came to visit our parents.

We already had said goodbye to both sets of parents the day before; it had been very hard, of course, but I was determined that I was going to remain strong and positive. Nonetheless, it was very hard seeing them so upset and I admit to feeling very guilty. I think we both did, but this was what we wanted to do and reminding ourselves why helped us both immensely.

We drove down on the Saturday before the move, staying at the Casterbridge Hotel in Dorchester - this had become something of a second home. The removal men were to follow on Monday and would head straight back again the same day. That would be a very long day for them but there were three of them and they would take turns to share the driving they assured me when I learned they would be doing it all in one day. They were so helpful, working tirelessly to complete a very professional job, for which we were most grateful.

# CHAPTER TWENTY-THREE

We were in our new home at last! It had all gone to plan, executed to absolute precision. This was Paul's domain: he would always plan everything to the finest detail; of course, as a project manager, planning was his day job and something at which he rather excelled.

We spent the next few days busily unpacking and settling in; it was a lovely house with a wonderfully open front aspect, looking onto the school playing fields. Ironic really as at the house we had just left the back gate opened onto school playing fields and then straight onto the sea. We also went out to explore some of the area a little as Sarah and I really hadn't seen very much outside of Dorchester; we'd only been there for the odd weekend, and then we were busy house hunting and getting a feel for the town. We all loved the place it immediately felt like home.

I took Sarah to school on the first day and went back home to do some more unpacking. I then decided I would have a walk into town to mooch around for myself and find my way. I bought some things for Sarah's bedroom to make it a bit more special as I knew that at some point, she was going to miss Barrow and little things like this would help. I knew I would, too, but we wanted her to feel secure and at home, here so whatever I could do to make it 'special' for her I would.

She was such a lovely happy girl and I wanted to protect her as any caring parent would. I loved and adored her so very much, I thought she was just perfect – my lovely Sarah Jane.

As it turned out, Sarah settled in incredibly well; she loved her school and had quickly made some nice friends. Her best friend, Emma, was a lovely girl and had taken Sarah under her wing and looked after her. Paul was happy in his new job, too. I was so happy. It couldn't have gone better. What more could I ask?

During the first month, I had found a little part time job, 12 hours a week, to fit in with school times. I hadn't planned to do that, but in a way the job found me when I saw the ad in a shop window as I was familiarising myself with the town. I went in, having seen a lovely dress in the window, and ended up being offered the job. That evening I told Paul about my, day as we always did, and he was very pleased and proud of me, another positive step in our transition. This really was all turning out even better than planned.

Despite having regular weekly telephone conversations with our respective parents, which inevitably ended with mine both in tears, they gradually seemed to be adjusting to things and had separate visit from both sets of parents within the first few months. They really liked the house and area and were finally all happy and relieved, I am sure, that we had settled so well. You might even say they appeared to approve at last.

Within a few months, we were all ship shape and organised and it was blissful. I did for a while find the pace of life so much slower than home; speaking of which, I had to regularly check myself as Dorchester was now 'home'. But I soon got used to it. I did get to thinking we should maybe have done this sooner as everything really did feel so right. That said, we had been so busy and I think it fair to say we were feeling tired and in need of a holiday.

Paul didn't ever like the heat, so he was always wary of going to the sun so he sadly never had been too adventurous or enthusiastic about holidays abroad to begin with; other than for our wonderful honeymoon we hadn't been anywhere and this was something I was by then longing to do. I wanted to take Sarah on a plane, to see another country and experience flying and exploring. The following month we went to Spain with Diane and her family to stay in Marbella on the Costa del Sol. They had swapped their timeshare week and so they kindly invited us along; it was all agreed and arranged very quickly.

The flight was short and most enjoyable and we touched down to a delightful sunny 24°C. We collected a hire car and made our way to the apartment, which was gorgeous and benefited from a private pool. For our entire stay, we enjoyed super weather with plenty of sunshine, a slight occasional breeze, brilliant blue skies and a few sporadic showers. The climate, the place, the people, the food; everything was perfect and I felt like I had gone to heaven.

On our second day we went for a walk around Puerto Banus, which had opened in the early '70s and whose guests had included the Aga Khan, Roman Polanski, Hugh Hefner, Prince Rainier and Princess Grace of Monaco. It was an amazing place to see, together with all the luxury yachts, some of which were owned by many famous names including Rod Stewart and Michael

Douglas. I just wasn't aware such places and lavish lifestyles really existed.

I had been well and truly bitten by the holiday bug and was already talking about where we should go the following year. We had joined a consortium with our timeshare, which enabled us to swap as Diane had done. So, the following year we went to Tenerife. We went with Paul's mum and dad, as my parents would never attempt to fly, Dad especially. It was a wonderful holiday but even hotter than Spain, which I didn't mind although Paul's Dad found it hard to cope with so he spent most of his time indoors during the day reading and sleeping.

Life in the south just seemed to get better really; yes, of course, I had my little moments when I missed family and friends and having days out in the lakes. But those moments never lasted and we did manage to go up to visit everyone quite regularly and maybe spend time picnicking in Ambleside or Windermere, or visiting places Ullswater, Kendal and Keswick. We would stay with Diane and Alan in Penrith, which was always lovely, and it helped to cope with those little moments of homesickness.

In 1992, Barrow underwent a vast, much needed and long-awaited improvement scheme, with a new shopping centre – Portland Walk – being built. At the time, it was the second largest shopping centre in the North West (the first largest being the Lanes in Carlisle of course and the third largest the Westmorland Centre in Kendal. It comprised thirty-three new stores, along with other areas they had developed and tidied. It was on one of our visits there only a year after our move that we saw it in its full glory during a visit to Diane and Alan.

It was also the year that we learnt that Paul's Dad had sadly taken ill. Paul and his Mum rang each other religiously every Saturday morning at nine-thirty; it had been a ritual since we moved and that morning was his turn to call her. We were about to have a little breakfast so he made a rather brief call just to say hello, but came off the phone feeling something was not quite as it should be. He said she'd sounded different somehow; he couldn't quite put his finger on it. He had asked if she was OK and she'd tried to reassure him she was, but he felt uneasy and within half an hour, he had made the decision to make his way to Barrow for a flying visit to show his face and from Penrith it was only just over an hour's drive.

He said he would be back to join in with our plans of a walk that afternoon and left just before ten, taking Sarah Jane with him. He was happy for me to stay and go out with Diane as we both had planned and by that time, he convinced himself that she probably had bit of flu or something, so he said for me to stay.

Diane and I had some breakfast together, dressed and just as we were about to leave I called Paul's mum's to check they had arrived safely as they should have been there. There was no answer. Maybe they were in the garden, I thought, so off we set for a nice girly morning together and had a lovely time as we always do. I bought a few little bits of make-up and accessories from Swaby's in Angel Lane, a shop I particularly liked to visit.

When we both were finished, we took the car back home and decided to go to the Clifton Hotel for lunch together, which was a two-minute walk from their house. I checked my watch and saw it was almost one o'clock and rang Paul's mum's to check what time they'd left so we would wait for them to get back so we could be together. Again, there was no reply; they must have popped out, I guessed; perhaps she needed something from the shops.

Diane and I went anyway and had a light lunch. It was very quiet in the Clifton and it wasn't the nicest of places, a bit tired and dated really and well overdue a makeover. However, it was clean, the staff were lovely and the food was rather good. We set off back home at two o'clock and I expected Paul to be back. As we entered the drive, we could see his car still wasn't there but thought he would be here soon. Three o'clock came and went and still no sign of them; I was by now starting to get rather worried. I tried to call once again but there was still no reply.

I now shared my concerns with Diane and she tried to assure me he would be fine. Gags was there with them and so maybe he was busy doing something with him, as he always found jobs to do for them and he did like to be kept busy. He was a lovely man and I thought the world of him. By five o'clock, there was still no sign or word at all and I could feel myself welling up. By that time I was imagining all kinds of things. He surely would have rung; I knew he would; he knew that I would be worried so why didn't he just call? I went upstairs and tried to distract myself by deciding what to wear that evening to go out and by ironing Sarah's clothes for her, as she would need to change. I got my new make-up out, put it on the bed, along with my new earrings and went back down stairs trying to remain positive.

Diane was in the kitchen finishing her last bit of ironing and she knows me so well so knew I was still concerned. I went up for a bath at quarter past six and washed and dried my hair and back into the bedroom when I heard the back door close and Paul's voice trailed up the stairs. What a relief, I thought, my heart pounding. I sat on the bed, opening my new eye make-up and heard him ask where I was. Diane told him and he came tearing up, rushed into the bedroom and fell at my feet. He buried his head in my lap and began to sob. He was shaking and crying so hard he couldn't speak, not a single word.

I was by now naturally very worried as never before had I seen him cry, not once in almost fourteen years. I stroked his hair and held him tight when he looked up at me like a lost little boy.

"It's my dad," he said. "Oh Sue! He has cancer," and started to cry again. I was in shock and thought I had misheard him at first, but I clearly hadn't. I don't know how but I found strength from somewhere. I couldn't fall apart, he needed me and I had to be strong; my husband was in pieces and I'd never witnessed anything like it ever from him.

After he had eventually calmed down a little he told me the whole story, apologising for not answering the phone; they had all been too upset and had not wanted to tell me over the phone, which was also why his mum hadn't told him that morning. These things should be done face to face if possible so he'd waited until he returned. He had also had Sarah Jane to consider, but she had been of great comfort to him.

It was dreadful news and as Paul went on to explain, it sadly had turned out to be terminal and that he had no more than six months to live; the cancer was in his liver now and was a secondary cancer so there was no hope for him at all. This was tragic; I was now feeling numb and didn't know what to say so I just held him in my arms for what seemed forever. I sent him to freshen up in the shower whilst I went down to tell Diane and Alan, as by then they had guessed that something was very wrong. It came as a great shock to them both as they were both very fond of his parents whom they knew very well.

We obviously didn't go out now as we had planned and decided to stay indoors and order a take away. None of us was really in the mood to eat anymore; the hunger I felt half an hour ago had disappeared completely and most of the food was left in the cartons to congeal overnight.

Paul and I got up early the next morning as neither of us had slept very much. We packed our things and decided we must go back to Barrow together to see them and would plan stay with them overnight. I would phone our respective employers on Monday morning, as we wouldn't be going into work for a few days at least. It was a very hard, quiet and sombre drive back that's for sure. Sarah was an angel, as ever, although she too was terribly upset. I was so pleased that he had taken her with him yesterday but now that regretted I hadn't gone with them.

This was so difficult to deal with and I don't know how but you do find an inner strength somehow; from where it comes I have absolutely no idea but it does and it was fortunate indeed because we all needed it then, especially Paul and Mum, to cope with this devastating news. We stayed over until Tuesday and did what we could, which in hindsight was not much. What can you do in these situations? Sadly, nothing except be there with them both. We would be back next weekend and the one after for as long as was possible and whenever they needed us.

It was a very difficult few months. We visited and stayed as much as time and our jobs would allow us. He fought bravely and courageously and his strength so humbling. His refusal of chemotherapy and other treatment, however, meant that we were waiting for it to happen. It was the hardest thing I had ever been through, watching someone dying in front of your eyes; the feeling of such helplessness is so incredibly demoralising. He didn't deserve this; he was a lovely man and a dear father-in-law. He sadly he passed away that August, a little more than five months after being diagnosed.

At last, he was at rest now and free from pain and suffering. That was now left for the family to deal with, especially poor Mum. The funeral was arranged and we all did as best we could under the circumstances. He had a wonderful send off at the church where Paul and I were married. No service of any kind would be right held anywhere other than St Mary's. Paul's family had always been regular church-goers there and, in fact, Paul had been a server there for many years. The church was completely full, every pew and I'd never before seen so many people inside that lovely building.

Paul and I had Mum to take care of now and to keep an eye on as much and as often as the distance would allow. It was difficult but we all coped. She would come to stay with us quite regularly and we would go off together for little breaks. She kept herself busy at home and the church, including helping out at the old people's home across the road. She had always had so many friends who were now especially important for her.

She is a unique woman and a tough cookie. I have never known anyone quite like her; I'm not sure I ever will.

# CHAPTER TWENTY-FOUR

Life goes on, as they say, and time is a great healer. You have to make adjustments in your life but you also eventually have to move on and learn to accept and adapt to new situations, in particular those that are thrust upon us without warning however hard and difficult they may be.

Paul was really enjoying his job; he travelled around quite a lot and worked long days at times but he seemed very happy which was most important. He was so like his father in many ways and the older he got the more obvious that became. They had been good together and, though they'd had their disagreements or differing opinions, that's all part of life and to be expected. He missed him more than I think he would really admit and he never really seemed to find it easy showing his emotions.

We started to have a few more holidays and the timeshare had opened up more options for us to travel abroad for a week in the sun each year. Paul, just as his father did, would sit in the shade on the sunbed in shorts and t-shirt with a towel covering every part of his legs (his feet always burned, despite all his attempts to avoid it). I used to find it quite amusing what he would wear in such heat but he just was not happy at all in the sun, unlike me. On this, we were so different.

I love my holidays and all the preparation and build up. I always want to be looking forward to the next one. I believe it gives me a focus and something to work and save towards and finding them and planning them is all part of the fun for me. I can spend hours quite happily surfing the internet (or Ceefax on TV in the old days) to find a great deal and have not failed yet. If there's one thing better than a fabulous holiday, it's knowing that you got a bargain!

Holidays are like most things in life, a matter of personal preference. What one likes another may not, but for me seeing new places and countries, how they compare, and the different ways of life, food, fashion and culture are all of special interest. Unlike Paul. He was very choosy and picky about where he would go and the temperature was a big influence. I always say if you go somewhere and don't enjoy it then you don't go back, but at least you have tried it. I am a big believer in not being put off visiting a place by someone else's opinion; you have to find out for yourself first hand.

Cruising had suddenly become a big favourite for us. What a wonderful way to spend a holiday, waking up in a different country each morning, comparing cultures and way of life, new surroundings, people, dress and fashion, décor, everything. It's all so enchanting and intrigues me still each and every place I visit, be it for a day or for a week or two it is a simply wonderful part of the experience.

The Caribbean was not only one of my ultimate favourite cruise destinations, but one of the best holidays ever. We spent two weeks over the Christmas and New Year period, with Mum and Sarah Jane, visiting the most amazing places including Tortola, St Kitts, Jamaica,

Mexico, Havana, St Maarten and Grand Cayman Island. I was in awe as each place was packed with its own individual beauty and identity, colour and personality. I really could have stayed on board for a month and even then probably not want to disembark.

It never ceased to surprise me though how many people on board complained, "It's not like Christmas is it?" What were people really expecting? You're on a cruise ship in the Caribbean in December with glorious wall-to-wall sunshine all day. What did they really think it would be like? If you want a traditional Christmas, then the Caribbean is not for you. It is hardly rocket science is it?

We enjoyed doing so many different things, from rolling a cigar in Havana and photographing the many classic cars to swinging on a hammock on the beach in Mexico; from walking on seven-mile beach to driving along some of the unkempt streets of Jamaica that were so full of character and history. There were so many places and memories that I would find it very hard to say which place I preferred as I loved them all; everywhere had its own individuality and personality. Then that is just typical of me – I love everywhere really. However, there are two places I had always been desperate to visit, namely Australia and Turkey. Two extremes, I know, but "must do's" without a doubt for me, although Paul never seemed overly keen on either, especially not Turkey.

Mum and I enjoyed a few cruises on our own, which was lovely. We did have great fun and always got on extremely well. She used to love the walk into the dining room on all cruises – she called it Walking the Gauntlet – but she loved the attention received by the crew and in particular the waiting staff upon entering the dining room to be shown to our seat. She was really good company and such great fun.

As with all good things that must come to an end, before you know it the holiday is almost over and you are packing to come home. However, planning the next holiday is always at this time already on my mind.

Our house was looking lovely and we had the garden looking very pretty, too, once again with Mum's help and knowledge for flowers and colour along with timings for planting. Thanks to her I was picking up lots of great ideas myself. The border around the back garden was a profusion of vibrant colours with the tall-growing Delphiniums fronted by Phlox, Iris and Lupins of various colours, with shrubs such as Ceanothus, Spirea, Cistus and Hypericum towards the rear. Trailing along and over the wall were delicate Clematis. It was beautiful and I was proud of what we had done with it over the last few years so we could now enjoy the benefits of all the hard work that we had put into it. I was very happy.

One day we heard the disappointing news that the Thomas Hardye secondary school opposite was closing and moving to the new building in Queens Avenue. The land had been sold to the same builders that had built our house. On the face of it, that maybe wasn't such a bad thing as we liked the house and had encountered no problems with it whatsoever. Neither were we against progress. That was until we saw the plans, in particular that there was to be house right in front of ours. This was not good news and even though it was likely to be eighteen months or more before the development reached that far, we really didn't like the idea of this at all.

Over the coming weeks we decided once again to move; we wanted to do it sooner rather than later as we were concerned on it affecting the price or selling potential. We had it valued within the week and put it on the market. I was so sad: this house more than any other was the one in which I felt most at home. I really loved it.

Within thirty-six hours, we'd received an offer and had agreed the sale. Paul had seen a house being built in the first phase of the new development and encouraged me to view it and if I liked it, we would go together. I wasn't too sure about the idea at first, as it was a mews house and in a terrace. I went the next day on my own and knew I liked it before I'd stepped into the hallway.

This house was much bigger than where we lived presently, had the benefit of a separate dining room (something I really would have liked), a study and a master bedroom en-suite. I wanted this house without any question of doubt. I knew we would all like it and was sure we would be happy here. It 'felt right'. I can't explain why it just did. We went together the next day and (as I knew he would) he loved it, too. Within no time, an offer was made and we had secured the place. About eight weeks later we had moved in, by which time almost everything was complete, leaving me just to choose carpets, curtains and all my favourite furnishings.

We had it all up together and ship shape in record time. I think after all the moves we'd made it had become second nature and we had become rather proficient at it by now, knowing exactly what to do to, when and how. There wasn't much about buying and selling we didn't know. I was always the one that could do the bartering and haggle a deal, if I thought there was one to be done, something Paul often congratulated me on as he admitted he couldn't and wouldn't ever do that. He was good at other things like meticulous planning and doing the finances. He was always planning, tapping figures into the computer and doing the accounting, balancing his spreadsheet.

So, in just a matter of a few short months, we'd moved from our wonderful house and garden in Highgrove Close to a spacious, brand new three-story mews house. Another new beginning.

# CHAPTER TWENTY-FIVE

Sarah was very happy and doing very well at school. It was amazing how much she had come on so since moving down to Dorset. She had joined St John's Ambulance with her friend Emma and loved it. She became very involved, joining in as an assistant at various events and shows, enthralled and excited if she had to help out with any casualty she may have been fortunate to assist with. She seemed to be growing up so fast and I was very proud of our little girl. I, too, was enjoying my little job in Etam and working with a lovely group the camaraderie was such fun. This was a lovely life and a very nice place to live. I was used to a gentler pace of life now and it felt like home.

Paul and I were at home one lovely August Saturday morning. We'd eaten breakfast together after I'd done my jobs and we were getting ready to go out for a drive when the phone rang. Paul answered it and handed it to me:

"It's for you – it's Diane."

Taking the phone from him, I spoke to her and I knew instantly from her voice that there was a problem.

"Hi, Sue, I've got something to tell you. It's George. He died in the early hours this morning. His partner had found him on the sofa, thought he was asleep and tried to wake him. When he couldn't he rang the doctor."

She didn't know much more than that right now but thought I should be told as soon as possible. I thanked her and put down the phone. Paul was standing at the door and I told him; he had the gist of the brief conversation but I confirmed that he had died. He said he was sorry but knowing our past asked me how I felt. I can honestly say I felt absolutely nothing! I kept saying to myself out loud, "He's dead. George my brother is dead." I knew I ought to feel something but I just didn't. The sympathy I felt was for my parents and nothing more.

We went out as planned and he took me shopping on the way and bought me a new dress. I don't think he really knew what to say or do as it was such a strange relationship that George and I had. But the more I thought about it I realised I suddenly felt a huge sense of relief. I know that must sound terrible, but I really did. I couldn't admit that to my parents, but I'm sure Diane and Phillip would have known and understood exactly how I was feeling.

They were both well aware our relationship was never good; they could see he had something against me, some kind of grudge, it seemed. Neither of them could understand why, no one could, unless it was perhaps some form of jealousy. Whatever it was, he had been horrible to me, and both Diane and Phillip had always been on hand to help dry my tears and dress my wounds, though I still bear the emotional scars to this very day.

It was two weeks before we could hold the funeral as Mum and Dad wanted George brought home from London, which was understandable but also quite a palaver. As the circumstances of death required a post mortem everything seemed to take forever. However, the day finally arrived and we all went up to the crematorium where a lovely service was held for him, with his favourite song being played in the background. I can't even remember what it was – probably Shirley Bassey as he adored her. Mum had insisted that it be played for him one last time, at which point I think everyone, bar me of course, began to cry. The service ended and the curtain started to close when both of my parents reached out and patted the coffin to say their last goodbye, holding tightly to each other. It was a tragic situation for them both to be faced with and I did feel so sad for them. You never expect your children to go before you.

We stayed on a few days following the funeral for support and help before making our way home again. It took them both a long time to come to terms with it, but I don't think they ever really got over it. I shouldn't imagine you ever do. I truly believe they always felt sorry for him; they always seemed to regard him differently, always worrying about him, Mum blaming herself for him being gay for some reason. I used to try to reassure her: "You cannot make someone gay, Mum. They are born that way and that's fine. It was nothing whatsoever to do with how you brought him up." I'm not sure she was ever convinced. I think she maybe just felt she needed to blame someone and it may as well be herself.

He was never talked about very much after this, at least not to me anyway, for which I was glad. For whenever he was discussed or even just his name mentioned, it made me shudder and stirred up many unpleasant memories and feelings. For me to talk ill of him to my parents when he'd died just didn't seem right, so I kept it all to myself, locked away inside. Even though he's gone, I still carry his wounds deep inside.

# CHAPTER TWENTY-SIX

The school in Dorchester was far better than the one Sarah Jane had attended in Barrow. It was a middle school system and was very different to what she had been used to so at times I worried her of finding it harder to adjust and settle. All my concerns were in vain. She was doing tremendously well and we were so very proud of how far she had come; this was of course a huge relief to us both. Her reports and results were wonderful, in fact faultless. She had taken it all in her stride and was achieving high standards but, most importantly, she loved school and it clearly showed.

One particular day, Paul and I had gone to Weymouth, as we liked to do on occasion. Before we moved down, Weymouth was a potential place to live, being a seaside town like Barrow. Now having moved to Dorchester, neither of us would want to live in Weymouth, although it is a lovely place to visit and virtually on the doorstep. We had been shopping and then went for a stroll on the seafront before deciding to head home.

The journey only took about twenty-five to thirty minutes, going through the villages and along the sea front. There was a slightly quicker way through the back roads but we didn't use it that day. When we stopped at the traffic lights at Upwey, Paul had his arm resting across the steering wheel waiting for the lights to turn green when I noticed something didn't look quite right with his arm. I leant across and gently stroked my hand over it and sat back again as the lights were changing. When he asked what I was doing I didn't say anything other than to say I thought he had a mark on his arm; I didn't want to worry him, certainly not while he was driving at least.

I couldn't help but feel uncomfortable about it; it was bothering me and I discreetly glanced at it again, but decided to wait until we got home so I would look at it properly. We got in the house and I made a drink; we took it up to the lounge and as I handed him a cup of tea, I took hold of his hand and led him to the window so I could see it properly. He smiled and asked again, what seemed to be so interesting. I pointed out to him the swelling I had noticed on one side of his forearm. He said he'd not noticed it before and seemed genuinely unconcerned. Well I was not so sure, but decided to leave it for now and to keep a close but discreet eye on it.

A few nights later, he was lying on the floor while we were watching the Simpsons. He had his head propped on this arm and was laughing aloud at as usual – he loved the programme, well we both did. I was sitting directly behind him and took a closer look. I hadn't mentioned it at all since the other day, but I didn't like what I was seeing. I was now becoming very worried, as it seemed to have visibly grown over just a couple of days. I waited until the programme had finished and I muted the TV; he turned to look at me and I simply said "Please will you go and see the doctor about your arm?"

"Why," he asked "are you really worried about it?" and he began to prod and poke at it.

"Yes I am. It may be nothing but I would really rather you had it checked out." I went down stairs to the kitchen as I had tears in my eyes and I didn't want him to see that and worry him.

We then watched the film, *The English Patient* (again) as it was Paul's all-time favourite film. I just wasn't taking it in; my mind was on him and thinking about what it could be. The next morning as he left for work I reminded him to ring for a doctor's appointment and told him I would if he didn't. Later that morning he called me to say he had an appointment booked for the end of the day, but only to see the nurse as all the doctors were fully booked. I wasn't too impressed but I thought if she had any concerns she would refer him herself so it was better than nothing.

I worried all day about him; he didn't want me to go with him as he really was convinced that we were wasting everyone's time. I waited and waited for him to come home. That day seemed like a week but eventually he came home. As I'd feared, the nurse had referred him immediately to see the doctor. The nurse had interrupted the doctor's surgery list and expressed her concerns. The doctor looked at it, felt it, poked and prodded it and admitted she was not happy with it at all. She couldn't say what it was, but said he needed to be referred to an orthopaedic consultant and that she would try to get him an appointment as soon as was possible.

I was very relieved that at least it had been checked, but also increasingly concerned as to what it might be. Paul never worried about anything health wise and rarely went to the GP for anything and I was so glad I had pushed him this time. About a week later, he received an appointment to see Mr Thacker at Weymouth hospital and naturally, I went with him. He had a scan and an X-ray and the result showed it to be a huge tumour. He needed to operate and quite soon as they couldn't say at this stage whether it was benign or malignant, but either way an operation was imperative.

My stomach was doing somersaults now but still he seemed so calm. He was amazing, which was a good thing as I was worrying enough for the two of us. I think he was trying to protect me as he knew how I must be feeling right now. He had to wait for the appointment to come through the post, but Mr Thacker assured us that it would be too long a wait.

Thankfully it wasn't, and he was soon given a date and the operation was performed successfully. The surgeon confirmed that it was indeed a huge tumour and that, as it had burst out freely when the incision was made and unconnected, it was thankfully benign. Had it not been checked and instead left alone it would have eventually burst the skin. The surgeon was surprised Paul hadn't noticed it earlier, when he admitted that somehow he hadn't and it was me that found it.

Paul now has a large and impressive scar as a result, far bigger than either of us had anticipated, sitting atop of his forearm, stretching from his wrist bone to the crease of his elbow. He laughed it off, saying it gave him a bit of character a kind of macho image, and said he would joke and tell anyone who asks that it had been the result of a shark attack.

I said he could make up whatever story he wanted to as far as I was concerned, I was just pleased for him that it was all over and he was going to be fine. However, he did end up being admitted to hospital urgently a few days later with an infection that could have proved very serious had it not been treated. He ended up being confined to the bed and stayed in hospital for five days attached to an intravenous drip of antibiotics and goodness knows what cocktail of medication. To this day whenever anyone mentions it to him, he jokingly says that I'd done it to him, that it was my fault as I'd made him have the operation. Then he cheekily winks and smiles at me, saying he was so glad I did make him go and see the doctor. He'd never have had it not been for me.

The scar has since faded a little with time, certainly compared to how it had been, but it's still clearly visible. That's a small price to pay in the grand scheme of things, as it could have been far worse.

# CHAPTER TWENTY-SEVEN

With Sarah being so happy, settled at school and growing up so fast, I became aware that I had more time on my hands. I wanted to work a few more hours so I decided it was perhaps time for a bit of a change and had just started to look for something different when I saw an advert for a cashier in a local bank. I'd done the end-of-day until balancing in the shop, but somehow that didn't seem comparable to what I imagined this role to require. After giving the matter some serious thought I decided to apply; even just completing the application form and hopefully making it to interview stage would give me some good experience until I eventually found something.

I applied, thinking I probably wouldn't hear any more of it, but pleased at least that I'd made a move in the right direction. I hadn't applied for a job in years, as the last one was literally handed to me on a plate when I wasn't even looking for one.

Two days later, I received a letter inviting me for an interview that same afternoon. I was stunned. It was just too good to be true, I thought. I hadn't even told Paul that I had applied, as I hadn't expected to hear anything. I remained calm whilst waiting, prepared for it as best I could and arrived five minutes before my two thirty slot. I was taken through to the waiting room in the bank and seated in a little side office until I was called. At two thirty prompt I was greeted with heart-warming smiles from two ladies, instantly setting me at ease, for, whilst I had been waiting I think momentarily I could have easily walked out again.

I sat before them both and they in turn asked me a number of questions that I answered confidently, honestly and to the best of my ability. I was given a description of exactly what the job entailed, along with what they would expect from me. I don't think it took more than twenty minutes or so before I was shaking their hands and leaving. I thought this may not have been a great sign, but I was happy that I had done my best.

The following morning at ten o'clock, the phone rang. "Hi, Sue" the voice began. "It was lovely to meet you yesterday. Thank you once again for your time and a successful interview. I am ringing to offer you the position, if you would like it. You can think about it overnight by all means, but I will need a reply tomorrow first thing, if you wouldn't mind."

I couldn't believe my ears; trying to appear calm, I said, "Well, thank you for the call and I would be very happy to accept." She was delighted and went onto kindly say that I had the job as soon as I'd walked into the office. I remember that they had both looked and smiled at each other when I'd walked in and I now knew why. What a lovely thing to say. I thanked her and finished the call.

To say that I was delighted is an understatement. I put on a CD, turned up the volume and was soon dancing around the house to Phil Collins, grinning like a Cheshire cat. I finished my housework in record time, dusting and hoovering whilst singing along to, 'Dancing to the light'. I was just so pleased and proud that I couldn't wait to tell Paul. I had done it! I really had been successful and it felt wonderful; such an amazing boost to my self-confidence.

That evening he walked through the door and I told him my news; he never was one to get overly excited about things, certainly not in any overtly demonstrative way, but he did seem pleased and that meant a lot to me. I handed in my notice; it was a four-week notice period, which was acceptable to the bank, so all was set fair. I was so happy.

Four weeks later and the day had arrived. I had woken up early, as I was terribly excited, with a tinge of nerves mixed in there, too. Somehow, this job felt different from my previous work; to me this was a 'proper job'. I was going to work in a bank, doing a responsible job. A proud, self-satisfied 'me' had herself a good, respectable and reliable job. I never would have believed I could have achieved such a position. I knew it was not rocket science, but it was better than stacking shelves or hanging clothes in window displays. I don't know why I'd doubted myself, but I had been full of doubt; nevertheless I had done it without any help from anyone at all, and it felt wonderful.

I arrived at quarter-to-ten as I was beginning my four-hour shift at ten o'clock but I needed to organise my uniform and undergo an introductory tour. After that I was introduced to everyone; it seemed a big branch, with so many people – I hadn't imagined what a large and varied workforce was employed there.

I soon settled in, learning the ropes quickly and getting to know everyone. I am very much a 'people person' and can get along with more or less anyone. Like anyone else I can sometimes have the odd personality clash, but I can more than handle myself should it be required.

It was a lovely place to work and with really nice people. My line manager – one of the two women who'd interviewed me – was wonderful. I soon got to know the customers, especially the regulars, so all combined it made for a satisfying and enjoyable occupation. The camaraderie was incredible, both at work and socially. Having a social calendar with work was something I'd not experienced. In most places I'd worked in the staff couldn't wait to walk out and go straight home. There's nothing wrong with that, but having such a busy social scene outside work really made me feel part of a team and not simply just a member of staff.

My twenty hours a week was just perfect; had I worked many more hours I wouldn't have enjoyed it half as much. Thankfully, we were in a financial position where I didn't need to work full time, Paul being well paid as well as very astute at controlling the finances. I was soon achieving all that what was expected of me and had even taken on a few additional responsibilities. The job was so satisfying.

Colleagues came and went, as they often do, moving onwards and upwards, or leaving the bank. It was quite noticeable that people didn't stay for years and years doing the same job – this was very much a place for the career-minded. Some would seek and take promotion in their stride, which is most admirable. One or two would become a little egotistical and arrogant, both behaviours I detest. I had the misfortune of having to work closely with one such person for a while. I found that calmly and assertively putting them in their place was not only very satisfying, but did actually improve our working relationship afterwards.

I had been in the job for over two years and still very happy indeed. That was until our lovely boss announced that she was moving on, an event that that filled the place with a noticeable air of despondency and dread. She was not only an amazing boss, but also a very entertaining and funny person. She always seemed to have a comedy anecdote, one liner or a bad joke on hand. She could always make me laugh.

I would often go home and share her stories and antics, ending up in complete hysterics. She could turn any dull moment into sheer hilarity in seconds. I often used to say she should be on the stage as she could ad-lib brilliantly. In some ways, this talent was wasted doing her job here but I was so pleased she was there. It was just as shame she was leaving as I believed no one could replace her.

# CHAPTER TWENTY-EIGHT

It was a Sunday evening after a nice weekend at home and we were thinking about going to bed when the phone rang. When I answered it I heard my mum; she sounded rather tired and not quite her usual self. I could only just hear her as she was talking so quietly. "It's Mam. I'm sorry to ring so late but it's your dad. I'm afraid he's in hospital", at which point she broke down. My heart was racing.

"What is it, Mum? What's happened?" Eventually she managed to compose herself and continue.

"He has had a stroke and he really is very poorly." She kept apologising for being the bearer of such news, but I assured her I understood and she mustn't feel bad about it. I tried to calm her and said to explain in her own time what had happened. We talked only for a few minutes as she was obviously very tired, but I'd understood what had happened.

They had been watching the TV together with a cup of tea. Dad had gone to the bathroom in the advert break when she'd heard a thud; she called to him and got no reply so went to see him. She walked in to find him slumped over the bath. Mum had tried herself to move him onto the floor so he would be more comfortable than where he was. Amazingly, despite the shock, she managed to move him.

She then immediately called for the ambulance and within moments, it had arrived. By all accounts, he was not in a good way at all. They took them both to the hospital, 'blues and twos' all the way. Over the next couple of hours, they examined and had started to treat Dad before sending Mum home to rest, promising to inform her immediately if there was any change.

Once I put the phone down, I just fell to pieces; I was numb with disbelief. He'd suffered a couple of minor strokes a few years previously but he had been fine again after a day or two and we even learnt that he had suffered a mild attack without even himself being aware. Something told me that this time the recovery wasn't going to be so quick. We eventually went to bed after I had calmed down, although my head was pounding. We had decided that we would travel up first thing in the morning to see him. Paul had been working from time to time back in Barrow so it would be easier for him to manage his work whilst I was with Mum and Dad.

Obviously, I didn't sleep very well and we ended up leaving at three o'clock in the morning to allow Paul to go to work after dropping me at the hospital entrance, as I'd wanted to go alone. I had cried so much throughout the journey and felt like crap so decided to walk in the grounds for a few moments to stretch my legs and clear my head before seeing him. Mum had stressed on the journey that he was very far from being his normal self and that I should be prepared.

I walked into the ward trying to be positive and paint on a smile when I was approached by a male nurse. I must have appeared rather lost as he asked me where I was heading or who was I looking for. I explained that my Dad, James, had been admitted the previous evening. He took me straight through. Dear God, I was not at all prepared for how my poor father looked.

He was in a cot and desperately struggling to get out of it and lean forward to speak to me. He was almost unrecognisable. I just didn't know what to do; it was such a terrible shock that I hurried around the corner of the ward and stifled a scream. The male nurse from earlier saw me and ushered me into an office to console me. He asked me what I had been told. I said that it had been explained that he had suffered a stroke and that he looked strange but I hadn't been at all prepared for this. He sympathised, put an arm on my shoulder and said that Dad was a very sick man and that I needed to talk to a doctor so things could be explained.

I nodded, calmed myself and said I wanted to see Dad again, despite the feeling of dread in my stomach. I went back to the cot and he looked at me and I knew instantly that he'd recognised me – I could see it in his eyes. Oh my, he was such a complete mess; his face was twisted beyond recognition; his arms and legs were as though they didn't belong to him; each of his fingers seemed to be pointing in a different direction. He tried to hold my hand but couldn't manage it as his loss of co-ordination made it impossible. He was also making awful grunting noises as he tried so hard to speak to me. He couldn't.

He was wet and looked so unkempt which was so unlike him. Even at eighty-two, he had a full head of hair that was always so immaculately groomed, but not today. Of course this was to be expected, but because he was always so particular about his appearance, I felt so sorry for him; if he had been aware, there was no way he would have let anyone see him like this, no one at all, even me.

He had clearly suffered a massive stroke. Oh my poor father, he didn't deserve this, not at all. I stayed with him for some time, just stroking his hair, trying to talk gently to him and calming his wriggling attempts to get out of the cot. I could feel him pleading with me to help him it seemed, but he wouldn't be going anywhere for quite some time to come.

They had to come to sedate him as he was fidgeting so much and he needed to be kept as still and relaxed. He was still trying to talk to me, but it was like a small child asking for things in a way that only a mother can understand. I decided that my presence and his inability to communicate with me was upsetting and distressing for him so I decided to come away and leave him for a while.

I went to sit down in the next little bay and just broke down once again. I couldn't accept it, but it was happening and tragically so very real. I scolded myself to snap out of it and compose myself, as he needed me now to be strong; I didn't want to let him see me like this. That was my dad, my loving, adorable father in there and he couldn't even hold my hand, bless him. He was always so incredibly affectionate, displaying great signs of love with hugs and kisses and telling me he loved me every time he saw me. I knew that was what he was trying to do then but he couldn't. He did adore me, and my sister. If there were anything I would have liked right now, it would have been one of those huge enveloping hugs and kisses. No one could hug like him and I'd always felt so safe and secure in his strong and gentle loving arms.

The doctor came to see me, we went to a private room and I sat as he explained sympathetically what had happened and what was being done to help. He stressed to me that it had been a massive stroke, which by now that was obvious to me, and although he was in the very early days, the signs weren't great for a full recovery. They would, of course, do everything they could, monitor him constantly and would keep us informed. It was imperative that he was not upset or distressed for fear of another attack. I listened and understood clearly his concerns and with that, I went back briefly to see him. I didn't want him to see me, though, as he seemed more settled than before after they had sedated him. I blew him a kiss, whispered, "*I love you, Dad*" and left him to rest.

I went outside and broke down again. I had been there a few hours and I was by now exhausted, although I felt guilty for feeling that way. Nothing about me mattered, only that poor man, my lovely dad, was of any importance right now.

Paul came to pick me up again and I went then to see my mum. She hadn't realised we were there yet as I told her last night we would be leaving home sometime during the morning but as we'd set off so early I didn't want to disturb her for she must have been so tired. I worried about her now, too. She opened the door and was surprised but very pleased to see us. She started to cry immediately and I let her release it all.

Her friend that lived close by was with her; they had been friends since we moved onto the island over thirty years before and she had lost her husband years ago. It was nice that she had her and they were good company for each other. She made us a drink whilst Mum told me everything from start to end. When she'd finished I said that I had been in to see him and this shocked her. She had wanted to prepare me beforehand as best she could for what I was to see of him. It was clearly far too late for that now and even if she had seen me, first it would not have prepared me for what I had so tragically encountered that morning.

I said that I had spoken to a doctor who was very kind and sincere; he had been extremely concerned as to Dad's condition, but said that he was in the right place and they were taking great care of him. She just couldn't wait to get him better and home again with her, but this was going to take time, we all knew that.

Over the next few days we all agreed a visiting rota so as not to crowd and tire him as he was so sleepy and very poorly. Understandably they were very strict, with no more than two at the bed and then only for very brief periods. We of course complied fully. Four days later I was on my own and went to visit him alone. I always paused a moment at the door before going in to take a deep breath in preparation for what I may face. I'd done this every time since the initial visit and shock.

However this time I was very surprised indeed to see a marked improvement. I was stunned. He was sitting up in bed his hair washed and combed (not by himself of course) and certainly not how he would wear it I hasten to add, but I would see to that for him. He smiled at me, albeit a very crooked smile, but it was more a smile with his eyes. He did have lovely big blue eyes, something both my sister and I have always been told we'd inherited from him. He was so pleased to see me. Oh my goodness how happy I was to see this; he tried to talk but he couldn't manage it and he began to sob. I couldn't help but join in now as I knew I was crying tears of joy at his progress.

I gently dried his eyes and took his comb out of his top drawer. I held his face to comb his hair, just like he did when he brushed mine when I was little; he would put his hand under my chin and gently squeeze my cheeks to make my lips purse into a silly pout and lift my head to look him in the face while he brushed. When he'd finished he would bend down and kiss me and tell me he loved me and we always laughed afterwards. Today was a little playful payback time as I combed his hair the way he'd brushed mine.

He did laugh, but with his eyes, as no sound of any recognition came from his mouth. He took my hand and held it for a while; that in itself was progress.

"Now, Dad, that's *much* better," I said, although I didn't show him the mirror as his face was so distorted, even though that was vastly improved too. I changed his pyjama top and splashed on a little of his favourite aftershave. I felt much better as I knew it would be appreciated. At last I could see my Dad was slowly, bit by bit, coming back to us. Oh my goodness, I was so happy.

We came and went daily and I could see the improvement sometimes even within an hour. He would get very tired and did get impatient, but to me that was another sign he was getting better. By Saturday morning it was a treat to see him. I just prayed that tomorrow he could talk back somehow. I was the only one of us all that could understand what he was trying to say, whether in silence with the little gestures or with the various grunts he would make. My mum couldn't believe it as she just couldn't work out any of it, which made her a little frustrated but glad that at least I could make some sense of it. I had become his interpreter for everyone.

That Sunday morning, after the best night's sleep in a very long week, I prepared to go with Diane to visit Dad. We had taken a few extras for him and a new pair of blue pyjamas. Someone had brought him green pyjamas and he hated green; he was terribly superstitious of it, so I had discreetly taken them home the previous night as I knew he didn't like wearing them.

We arrived at the ward and made for his bed, which was a little closer to the door. He was lying down, facing away from us. Assuming he was asleep, I suggested we go to get a cup of tea and a magazine rather than disturb him. Off we set and returned twenty minutes later and he was on his back staring at the ceiling. We approached the bed and looked down at him and his eyes looked glazed. I spoke, he looked at me but there was barely a reaction. He began to weep again and I kissed him and dried his eyes.

"Are you going to sit up then while we tidy you up Dad? After all my work yesterday you've let yourself go," I joked and laughed. There was barely a flinch from him; my heart lurched as I realised he had failed dramatically in 17 hours.

We sat quietly with him and caught the eye of a nurse so I went out to speak with her. I recognised her as a friend from school; she had just returned from holiday so I'd not seen her before today.

"Can I have a word about my dad, James?"

"Yes certainly. I hadn't realised he was your dad." She then invited me into the office. "He had another little turn last night and we are just keeping a close eye on him, hence moving him to a bed nearer the door. It is very early days and he has made great progress, far better than we had imagined at this stage, so we shall just take it steady and keep him quiet for a few days I think. No more than one person at the bedside and then only for very short periods." I understood, thanked her and then made my way back to see him just lying there motionless.

We were there for most of the day and there was barely anything from him at all. I wouldn't leave him on his own so we relayed toilet visits and breaks so he wasn't alone in case he stirred or needed anything. Time passed and by 8 p.m. we were bushed. I left to go to the bathroom as Diane quickly nipped over to see the nurse at the doorway as she had just began her shift.

When we came back to the bed, he'd gone. Whilst he was alone and within minutes, my father had passed away. I felt so angry with myself that he was alone at the end but the nurse, trying to comfort us, said that he was a gentleman to the end and didn't want to die in our presence. Little comfort at the time, but I knew she meant well. We were devastated and we had now to tell Mum.

He suffered greatly, of that, I am sure, but eventually as hard as it was, I came to be thankful that his suffering was over. It had been a very long, hard week for everyone but for him especially. One week, almost to the hour, after it had happened and now, he was gone.

I am so very grateful of the little fun we had shared the previous day, that he'd held my hand and I am sure he'd almost spoken my name.

Mum had asked Diane and me to choose the clothes in which he was to be finally laid to rest, as had been requested by the funeral parlour. We knew he would want to be sent off looking his very best and both went through his wardrobe together. I think we chose very well indeed and there was plenty from which to choose that's for sure. His favourite blue jumper, a white long-sleeved shirt (he never wore nor owned a short-sleeved shirt) and a pair of blue-grey marl trousers. We made sure his best black shoes were polished to his high standards and selected his favourite and most important accessory, a blue and grey striped tie.

Diane and I took the clothes down to the funeral parlour and left them to get him ready. She wasn't too sure if she wanted to see him at first and I understood her slight hesitation, it isn't for everyone. I knew I wanted to see him, I simply knew I must. Diane did decide she would join me. We had to wait for them to prepare him so went back the next day to see him for the very last time.

We arrived, as arranged, at ten o'clock. Diane admittedly a little pensive and my tummy was churning too. We gathered ourselves, walked into the room and the first thing I noticed was his mass of steely grey hair. We slowly approached the coffin and looked in to see our Dad. He looked more like the man I remember; in fact, in some strange way, he looked a bit younger and more importantly he was now at rest. He looked so very peaceful.

I made a slight adjustment to his hair that wasn't quite right; after all it was his crowning glory and I owed him that just one last time. It was moving and admittedly difficult, but I wanted to see him at rest after a most difficult week and am so pleased I did so. I kissed his cold forehead and whispered, "I love you, Dad," then said to him what he had said to me without fail every night when he was tucking me into bed at home. "Night, night. God bless. I love you." I left him, with tears running down my face, feeling for the first time since he'd taken ill almost a sense of relief.

The funeral the next day went very well and was well attended, confirming his popularity. He was given a lovely send off, one he deserved and one of which he would have been proud. He wasn't perfect, not one of us are, but to me he was the best Dad in the world. It was a tragic end to his life but he is now at rest and free from pain; that's the best way for me to think of it and the way I managed to deal with it at the time and to this day. I just want to say again to him now, thank you, Dad, for all you did and said and for loving me so very much, just as I love you. I miss you every single day and night and think of you so very much. Night, night and God bless.

I wrote and placed this poem in his coffin the day before the funeral.

*Please save a place right by your side,*
*In your loving arms once more to guide.*
*We shall one day all be together*
*It's down to when and not to whether.*
*I know you're watching closely by*
*From that lovely place up in the sky.*
*Now just be good and don't be cheeky*
*And please just promise to not be weepy.*
*The time shall pass too fast I know*
*My love once more I then will show.*
*Good Night and God bless you, Dad.*
*I love you xx*

The following weeks were very difficult as I tried to come to terms with the loss of the man I loved so very much, the man who constantly showed me and told me how much he loved me. Those three words that are so simple but that mean so much from or to someone so dear. Those words that are in many cases not used nearly enough. It was also difficult to see my mum without Dad, to walk in the house and see her alone when for so many years they were usually together. They had their moments, but my father adored her; you could see it when he just looked at her, after all those years I could still see it. He didn't have to say anything, it was just so obvious. He always called her his beautiful lady. I often used to envy the love they had and after so many years for it to be still so strong.

We spent time sorting out all his belongings as it was clearly going to be too difficult for Mum to do although she felt it was necessary as she decided it would help her to move on. She felt she needed a kind of spring clean, not quite everything but most of his things out of the house; she said she didn't need to see or have his things all around, looking at her every day to remind her of him. She had all her memories of him stored safely away in her head and no one could ever take them away.

We came back home to Dorset and tried to pick up some kind of normality again but special occasions such as birthdays and Christmas when you receive a card just saying now 'Love from Mum' hits hard. After the first one or two you grow to accept it, you have to. Time heals but the pain never really leaves you, it just gets easier to deal with and you learn to adapt to the void of not having that person around.

We spent a nice Christmas all together that year at my sisters. Having Mum with us we made it as normal as it could be, which she appreciated very much. She was an independent woman and had said at first that she would be fine on her own and needed to get used to it. There was simply no way we could have done that and she clearly enjoyed us all being together under one roof celebrating the festivities. Dad was much talked about of course and fond memories were shared as we raised a glass to him, as I do now. I never forget to wish him Merry Christmas and tell him I love him each year that passes.

# CHAPTER TWENTY-NINE

The February after Dad had died Paul, Sarah and I went as normal to our timeshare at Cameron House on Loch Lomond where we would celebrate both Sarah's birthday and mine. That had been one of the main reasons for buying the week we did and it had been a wonderful investment. It was wonderful to be back there, gliding along the long drive into the estate on the southern shores of the loch. It's like being transported to another world for that week, a world devoid of any stress, worries or pressures.

When I arrive, I totally and utterly switch off, living in absolute luxury whilst enjoying all the local surroundings and walks. Loch Lomond is on the edge of the Trossachs, with the impressive Ben Lomond bearing down on the Loch from the north east, often topped with snow during our February week. Cameron House is also not very far from Glasgow, a great place for a bit of culture and architecture, or for a spot of retail therapy (usually on my birthday).

Whatever we've done during the day, it's so nice to be able to return to the estate for a swim and relaxing sauna before retiring to the comfortable and meticulously equipped lodge.

That particular week we had a gentle mix of sightseeing, walking and simple relaxation. It was just what was required after our first Christmas without Dad. As usual, when it came to the end of the week I left in tears. I get so emotional every single time we leave after a week of luxuriant escapism.

We got back home to Dorset and settled back into normal life again. A fortnight or so later we went back to Barrow to visit the family for the weekend and to help Mum with a few jobs. I went to my mum's and she was so pleased to see us, but was feeling a little under the weather. She tried to brush it off but I insisted she went to see the doctor, even though we guessed it was simply everything catching up with her and making her feel rather run down.

The doctor wondered the same thing initially so ran some tests to give her a bit of an 'MOT'. He also suggested some tablets to help her sleep as she was finding her brain so active in the night that she was finding it difficult to sleep. I was glad that she had seen him and was getting herself sorted. It's obvious that if you don't sleep very well for any period of time everything becomes such an effort and seems worse. At least now, she could catch up on her lost sleep.

I did a few jobs around the house and bought some food supplies as she couldn't carry too much and her dear little brown Fiesta was in the garage for repair. I left Mum, quite satisfied now but I still missing my dad sitting there in his chair, or hiding behind the door and jumping out to surprise me. I'm not sure I will ever really get used to his absence.

The following Friday I was busy cleaning my windows at home when the phone rang. It was my mum calling to telling me that she had received the results of her test. The news was worrying; they had done a scan on Wednesday and found cancer in her colon. I couldn't believe what I was hearing. She didn't want to tell me over the phone but living so far apart made it unavoidable. I tried so hard to keep it together and not cry on the phone, but she knew I was in tears.

Poor Mum. Less than four months after my dad had passed away and now she had this to deal with. Life can be so unfair and cruel. However, they said they had caught it early and the prognosis was reasonably positive; at least that was something. They planned the operation urgently for the following week to give her the best chance of a recovery.

Naturally we went back to see her and she looked radiant. Within a week she looked better than I had seen her in a long time; what a relief that was. Onwards and upwards, the doctors assured us; they had caught the cancer soon and had managed to remove it all. The usual checks would obviously be necessary and healing would take some time but they believed the operation had been a success.

The miracles these people can perform are incredible. I have tremendous respect and admiration for all our emergency services, in particular our doctors and nurses, for they truly do a tremendous job.

We visited her again a month later. I was with her, sat on the sofa having a cup of tea but she appeared to be in a great deal of discomfort. Immediately we got a taxi to the surgery. I wasn't leaving anything to chance and the doctor thankfully saw her straight away and examined her before deciding that he would refer her to the doctor who'd performed the operation.

He saw her just two days later and the sad conclusion was that the cancer had returned or maybe that they hadn't taken enough of the intestine away during the operation. She was simply not fit or well enough for them to re-operate, even if it had been an option. They tried her on a course of chemotherapy, which unfortunately she couldn't cope with at all; it made her so physically ill that they had to stop it after only the second course. I went with her for that and it was so awful to witness her pain and the vomiting she was suffering. So soon after my father's illness, the dreadful feelings of helplessness were all too fresh in my memory. I couldn't believe this was all happening yet again.

My mum was so brave, bless her, but we all realised she was terminally ill. There was no happy ending. She passed away peacefully just two weeks later; almost five months to the day after my father had died. It was all so tragic. I had barely come to terms with having lost my father and now I had lost my wonderful mother too. Why do these things seem to happen to the nicest of people? Life can be so very cruel.

One simple thing that did help me cope a little later was when someone told me that they thought that perhaps my mother just couldn't live without my dad and maybe it was more a broken heart that took her. We knew it was cancer, but I found some comfort in the sentiment; perhaps at these times you grasp at anything to help you through the situation. At least they were soon to be together once more, where they belonged.

There was once again another funeral for us to arrange and attend, so recently after Dad's passing. We sadly knew the routine and all that was necessary. But this time we would have to give up the house, losing that personal family connection with Barrow; this was a very strange feeling. I didn't regard the place as home anymore, nor had I for many years, but it was my birthplace, my husband's and our daughter's, and the place where we'd both met all those years ago.

Mum's funeral was in fact closing the door on Barrow for me; there were no personal family connections any more, except my brother, Phillip. In the aftermath of the funeral, Diane and I lost even that connection with Phillip, my lovely brother. I won't say exactly what happened, but jealousy has forever removed Phillip from our lives. You can sadly choose your friends but not your family.

# CHAPTER THIRTY

Paul, Sarah Jane and me had become so used to going back to visit his mother and the three-hundred-and-sixty-mile round trip was now part of our normal life. I often used to think the car would find its own way there. Now all was different and as much as I loved her, she wasn't my mum. It just wasn't the same anymore; Barrow felt different, everything felt different now. Every time I did go back it was like I was looking at the place through someone else's eyes; the family connection really had gone and the place seemed almost soulless somehow. I didn't feel like I belonged anymore and that seemed like another kind of loss in some strange way.

Once more, I learnt that time is a healer and I had begun to deal as best I could with the loss of both parents an inner strength prevails.

The Sunday ritual of us calling each other in turn had of course stopped and visits to the hometown reduced even more because Paul's mum would come and stay with us more regularly, usually for a month each time, so as to make full use of the month's validity on her train ticket. She had made friends with various people that she'd met at the church in Dorchester; she had also befriended some of our neighbours and in fact, some she got to know some even before I had. She had made rather a nice and busy life for herself over successive visits.

Despite feeling as if things were starting to settle to whatever 'normal' was, it was suddenly brought home how much it taken its toll on both Paul and I. One evening I'd been quietly thinking ahead, planning the evening meal when I turned to see him watching me. He had an angry expression and with a slightly raised tone, he burst out.

"What on earth is up with you? I can't stand this, Sue! Which one of us is going? You or me, because one of us has to leave!"

I couldn't believe it and hadn't seen it coming at all.

"I'm sorry," I apologised. "I guess I'm still grieving. It's all hit me so hard but I'm trying to get over it. And I'm not going anywhere."

He snapped back angrily,

"Well the door is right there!" I replied as I ran up to the bathroom, closed the door and began to cry. I just couldn't believe his insensitivity and I was furious. After a while I settled down and went down to speak to him, only to find he had gone out, sulking like a baby I didn't doubt, in fact his mum used to say that his dad was exactly the same. She said she had to work him around to get him to snap out of his mood swings but it could take days and she hated it. I was starting to understand just what she meant.

It was painfully frustrating and upsetting; I didn't know why or how he'd managed to change. I tried to imagine what had triggered it but to no avail. Perhaps I'd been somewhat quiet and insular, but hell, I was still grieving. It was then that I decided we desperately needed a holiday, some time together and some much-needed sunshine and relaxation.

When he eventually came home, we sat and talked about everything. I apologised, as I usually did, even when it wasn't my fault. I did so to try and avoid the moods going on for days. I couldn't do with that at all, not this time, not again. I'd had enough of the long days of silence and moody atmosphere; I'm certainly not perfect I can stress that, but it was unbearable, not to mention unnecessary.

Eventually we made up, sitting and talking into the evening before agreeing that a holiday was a good idea. In no time at all I'd found us a fabulous cruise deal on the internet, all-inclusive and with convenient flight times from the local airport at Bournemouth.

We spent a lovely week cruising around the Mediterranean. It was so good to relax and switch off. The boat wasn't the best in fairness; it was rather old and tired-looking if I'm honest. I do vaguely remember it being advertised as its farewell journey but thought nothing of it at the time. Nevertheless, the food and entertainment were outstanding and camaraderie with new friends delightful. The places we visited were most interesting, and the weather was simply first class. All in all, we'd desperately needed the time alone together and perhaps now we could start again.

# CHAPTER THIRTY-ONE

Sarah had long since decided that nursing was her vocation following her continuous and zealous enthusiasm for her St John's ambulance membership. Pretty much since enrolling at the age of nine, she had always shown such dedication and enthusiasm.

She talked so passionately about it when she came home from each class. Nothing she faced ever seemed to phase her and she coped with all kind of situations. We saw this ourselves first hand whilst attending and supporting her during various regional competitions that she'd been selected to take part in. I felt more proud than ever to see for myself her faultless confidence and ability in front of large audiences, even at such a young age.

She'd also done tremendously well at school; her final results were astonishing, achieving A's and A*s in every subject. She had worked tirelessly and the results were clear evidence of her hard work. For some time, she'd been researching universities suitable for the nursing degree she wanted to study. She'd visited a number of them with her father and had decided that Southampton was her first choice, dependent on getting the required grades. As she easily had the grades she needed, Southampton was confirmed as her destination in September.

I was now realising that the time was drawing ever closer to my baby going off to university, to begin her life as a student, without her parents close by. I wondered and worried how or even whether she would cope with student life, as she'd always been quite a home bird in many ways. She never really cooked or helped much with the housework (a cause of frequent arguments between us all) but I know this is not unusual behaviour for teenagers

She had lots friends and always seemed a popular girl. She'd dated the occasional boyfriend, one of whom had become quite serious in her final year of school, a lovely boy, but that ended after almost a year.

# CHAPTER THIRTY-TWO

Sarah leaving for University was undeniably a very hard step for me. I really wasn't looking forward to it. In fact, I'm ashamed to say I was dreading it. Moreover, I came to realise that I simply wasn't prepared for it at all; but how can you? There isn't an on-off switch to parenting, which is a full-time commitment for so long. Suddenly your baby isn't going to be coming home anymore at regular times, nor sitting at the table eating with you and talking about her day, nor kissing you goodnight and saying "I love you" as she goes to bed. All 'normality' is to change. How do you actually prepare for it?

Nevertheless, I knew I shouldn't be selfish about it and tried to keep a lid on it. I had to be strong and let her go off to find her own way in the world. However, I knew I was going to miss her more than I can say. I remember Paul's mum telling me many years ago that our kids are only on loan to us. Well I could hear those words loud and clear and was beginning to realise exactly what she meant.

So if I may say to anyone who is about to experience this now or at some point in the future, please at least try to prepare yourself as much as possible in advance as it can be mentally exhausting... and financially expensive as well!

As she grew older, Sarah became a most determined and strong-minded young woman. This was something I found rather challenging at times and difficult to deal with if I'm honest; in fact, both her father and I did. The beautiful, young and obviously very intelligent young woman whom I'd given birth to and nurtured now had her own opinions and we could no longer tell her what to do.

I'd always been the one to see her off to school in the morning and there to greet her every day she came home (I'd never wanted my child to become a 'latch key kid') and so I often received the initial download from her day at school. I always ensured my job and working hours would fit in with her and her schooling; I put her before anything and everything, which was one of the reasons why I was finding this so hard to deal with I guess.

Now my daughter seemed to have turned almost overnight into a young woman, one with her own mind, ideas and dreams. She no longer seemed to need me in the same way anymore. Without trying to sound too melodramatic, the realisation had dawned that I was rapidly becoming a redundant mother. What did I do now? Perhaps I should have listened to Paul's Aunt Hilda who had more than once encouraged us to have another child.

Aunt Hilda, I should point out, had only one son and he had been tragically killed in a motorbike accident at the age of twenty-one. She never really got over and I think that is why she tried whenever she saw us to encourage me to think seriously about having a second child. However, I was stubborn; I just couldn't do it and was still terrified after all these years of becoming pregnant again, or more importantly the birth. If there were one thing I could turn the clock back and change in my life it would be that we should have had a second baby.

There is no one way to raise a child, no hard and fast rules. You just learn to do it as best you can, together, learning from each other and how and what suits your personal feelings, ideas and beliefs, gradually transferring your values to your child, in the hope that they eventually turn out to become a good, well-rounded person.

Yes, I made mistakes and I tried to learn from them. How we deal with our mistakes shapes both our children and ourselves. I admit to being overprotective with her whenever she was ill and I always worried about her health. Better to be safe than sorry, so a trip to the doctor for reassurance was more than worth it for the peace of mind.

It's only my opinion, but I believe Paul and I did a very good job with Sarah Jane. I believe that raising a child together is one of the most important and rewarding things two people can ever do together. Of course, it can at times be demanding and challenging, but it's something that can also bring you closer together as a couple. For some I know the reverse can be the case, but Paul and I were close, caring and loving parents. I think if you were to ask Sarah, today she would agree.

And so the day had arrived: Sarah's A-level results had allowed her to get her place at her first choice of university, so she was Southampton-bound at eighteen years of age. She was entering the big wide world, going to a place where she knew nobody. No one in either of our families had gone to university, which made it an even more special moment for us all, but which also revealed our ignorance of what lay ahead.

We packed the car with all her essentials and more besides, but somehow managed to jam ourselves in amongst it all. How many other families were going through the same ritual? The journey seemed quite long; my tummy was doing summersaults and my emotions were all over the place.

I'd promised myself that I would not cry; I had to be strong for her if nothing else. Eventually we arrived at a huge and imposing building, with labyrinthine corridors and stairways that seemed to go on forever. We eventually found her room, opened the door and my stomach dropped. I stepped into a little room with a half decent wardrobe and chest of drawers that had clearly seen better days, and a single bed with a mattress that had suffered goodness knows what in its time. I had to step outside a moment and compose myself so made the excuse I needed to visit the bathroom. I thought it was going to be tough for her as she certainly liked her home comforts, but this was her choice and I couldn't say anything. I was trying so hard to keep myself calm for her sake, I then went back in.

We unpacked everything from the car then sorted and settled her into this little room on campus. It overlooked a courtyard with an area of lawn which I thought was rather nice and I imagined her sitting there on a rug in the sun, reading and chatting to her new found friends. At least this made me feel a little happier for now.

The clock was ticking and the time had come for us to leave her; she clearly was chomping at the bit to get on with it and meet everyone. So we took our leave, I gave her a kiss and she walked back to the car parked just outside the gate with us. I climbed in the front, closed the door and said quietly, "Just drive off quickly please, Paul."

I hesitated at first but couldn't resist looking in the wing mirror to see her and she wasn't even looking back; she carried on walking back through the gate and out of sight. It was at this point I just let go of all my emotion and burst into tears. I can see her now as clear as anything in her beige top and jeans wearing her beautiful hair in a loose ponytail, disappearing through the gate, a most poignant memory that will stay with me forever.

That for me was the point in which I realised I'd lost her. That was the day she left home, never to return, at least not to live anyway. I will admit that I frequently went into her bedroom, empty of most of her personal belongings, to lay on her bed crying into her pillow. Doing so tormented me, but in a strange way, it also helped, because I could smell her and feel that she was close. I can't describe how much I was missing her.

Naturally Sarah settled in very well indeed and made lots of new friends and was, as ever, a popular girl. She now had a completely new and different life. One or two of her acquaintances in the hall of residence had dropped out because they couldn't hack it for one reason or another, but not Sarah-Jane.

She had only been there for her 'Freshers' week when she met a guy called Mark. She told me about him on the phone and said she wasn't interested in a relationship, but they'd had a few drinks together and appreciated him as a friend. As you might imagine, before long they'd starting going out and things happily progressed from there. I was worried about the distraction it might cause to her studies, but fortunately this proved not to be the case.

I could write endlessly here about her university days and what I learnt about it from her (or at least what she'd been willing to share with me) and life therein as to how it was for me and for her. However, there is one episode in particular I shall share is that we did have an extremely traumatic and worrying month in particular with her I'm afraid.

Whilst at university, she'd had to go into hospital for a routine operation on the day surgery ward. The operation had been postponed a few weeks previously due to her having a cold; she had been admitted but on discovering her cold (as well as her asthma), they refused to operate and sent her back home straight away. On her second visit, she was admitted and they did perform the operation as planned; I took the train to visit her during the late afternoon after the operation. As expected, she was groggy, tired and listless.

The nurse had just delivered a sandwich to her as I arrived on the ward as she hadn't eaten anything all day, I was told. She wanted none of it, refusing it, saying she just didn't fancy anything at all as she felt so poorly. She started to cry and did look very poorly; she couldn't even manage to sit up in bed she was so weak.

I tried unsuccessfully to get her to eat but and had to give up. I stayed with her a while but she was just sleeping, so I headed back home again to Dorchester on the train. Both her dad and I went the next day to visit, expecting that she would be discharged, but when we arrived to find that this was not to be the case. We found her to be just as I'd left her the previous day, in fact I thought a little worse.

I spoke with the nurse who said she still hadn't eaten very much. She had tried a sandwich earlier but couldn't keep it down very long and threw it all back again. They were starting to worry about dehydration, so I tried as best I could to get her to drink, but within no time, she was throwing it all back again.

We were of course now becoming very concerned indeed, as to exactly what the problem was, as to me it seemed very serious. A doctor came to see her and decided that they would move her to over to the general hospital to be assessed by the health care team there. This happened quite quickly, and they did various tests, the results for which would come back the following day. Eventually we left for home but went back early the next day to visit and I was horrified to see how ill she was.

She was losing weight as for three days everything she swallowed was immediately projectile vomited. We were by now seriously worried about her. What was more worrying was that they couldn't seem to find the underlying cause of the problem at all.

After almost a week and numerous test and different doctors, still no answer. We had gone to visit this day and she wasn't in her bed, my heart was now racing. I frantically went in search of a doctor to ask some serious questions when she suddenly arrived back on the ward.

We were taken to one side and they admitted that they were all becoming increasingly worried about her and were still none the wiser as to her condition. I broke down and angrily shrieked, "*Please* just find someone that can help her! Just look at her!" for she was, by now, so very thin, weak and frail. It was heart breaking to witness.

The worry of this was seriously affecting both Paul and I. Our own GP, Doctor Riddoch, was again incredibly supportive to us both during this awful time, for which we were truly grateful.

Eventually, back in Southampton, a consultant called Mr Beck ordered a scan to be carried out so he would assess the results to see what it showed but again there was nothing obvious. So he asked for our permission to operate to investigate further; this was far from an easy decision but we decided that we had to agree in the hope of finding out what was wrong. The operation was performed after midnight that night and we both sat outside the operating theatre and nervously waited and waited.

The news finally arrived that he had found that her bowel had been perforated during the initial operation. Apparently, the organ 'sulks' if handled, for want of a better description, therefore as she tried to eat, everything was just hitting her stomach and coming straight back out. I couldn't believe this appalling news; I was furious, but we were so relieved that he had the answer and was confident that even though she was far from well, her chances of a full recovery were hopefully very good. This was now a waiting game and over the next few days, we should see a marked improvement.

Thankfully, we did and she gradually got stronger, started to eat and drink and keep it all down. Slowly she began to gain weight. This was one of the most difficult, traumatic and worrying times of our lives, and one I know for sure we shall never forget. We owe so much to Mr Beck of Southampton Hospital; we thanked him from the bottom of our hearts for saving her and we shall never ever forget him.

Happily, the rest of her time at university was comparatively uneventful. There were highs and lows and enough tales and stories to fill another book, but let me simply say that she went on to be proudly offered a place in the hospital in Southampton during her last year. Her graduation day was one of the proudest days of my life. She and Mark had become very serious, but the relationship had not affected her studying at all, as I'd first feared. In fact, Mark had been a tremendous support for her.

Her aptitude for studying didn't stop there, however. She was like a human sponge and just loved learning. We went to visit her one day and she appeared somewhat distracted. After a bit of a wait and with her Grandma at her side, she announced that she wanted to leave the hospital. Briefly, my heart sank before she went on to explain that she wanted to further her career and study to become a midwife. I was suddenly overjoyed and proud at this announcement. She had managed to secure a place at Guildford University to study a midwifery degree.

For the record, I did eventually come to terms with her leaving home. I still missed her, of course, but I managed to settle and relax in the confidence that she was happy and had many new friends. In all honesty, going to university had been the best thing she could have done.

The way she took all these new challenges and experiences in her stride means to me that her dad and I had done a good job nurturing her and encouraging her constantly to do her best. It's Sarah, however, who has done all the hard work; she is a credit to herself and I thank her and admire her for everything she has achieved, and for continuing to make me the proudest mother in the world.

# CHAPTER THIRTY-THREE

Life had changed quite significantly for both Paul and me over quite a short period. Both my parents had died as well as Paul's father, Sarah had left home and was settled with a great career ahead of her. She loved her job and had a lovely boyfriend who took great care of her. They were now also very happy living together in a super flat they were renting. For me as a parent these were most satisfying feelings. I realised I no longer worried about her now, well at least not in the way I had over the years when she was at home.

I suddenly found I had time to think about me; my life and where I was. This was all quite new to me it was something I had never done, I got lost in thought in this unfamiliar territory.

For so many years, I'd seen myself first as a wife, then a mother and a homemaker. Now things were different; I got to thinking that I should maybe consider a career, or maybe trying something different within the bank where I was now. They always asked those kinds of questions at year-end appraisals, or when other opportunities arose within the company, but I had never really bothered before. I'd always felt that my job didn't really matter that much.

I'd always encouraged and supported Paul with his job and if he wanted to do anything to further his position then I would do whatever I could to support him (just as I had in the past when we'd moved down to Dorset). However, Paul's job was always just that, a job. He never really considered it a career, as such, he was never that way inclined or motivated and that was fine. We would often talk at length about it in the evenings: should he or shouldn't he pursue something that was being advertised internally that could be considered a potential step up for him?

I positively encouraged his progression whenever he was at all inclined to do anything about it, but it wasn't very often. That's not a criticism of him. How could I? I was exactly the same with my job. He simply never aspired for a senior role, which was where the money was, and he liked it that way.

I had never seriously thought about my future or me at all. I guess in hindsight I felt like I was a secondary as my jobs were always just a kind of 'get me out' and to help with extra savings, as well as a bit of pocket money for me. I had jobs at home too, taking care of the house and the cooking and cleaning.

My 'job', first and foremost, had had to fit in and around Sarah-Jane. Perhaps that's a little old fashioned, but there is nothing wrong with that and it was the way Paul and I worked together as a team which in turn allowed us to do what we did and achieve all that we had. We didn't want to pay child-minders or strangers to look after our daughter, to miss her all day, to pick her up in the evening to bath her and put her to bed. So it had always been imperative that we were there for her as much as we could, me especially.

Now that Sarah was settled however, I found myself giving my career some serious thought. I considered enrolling on a course locally to do interior design, as that is a great passion of mine and always has been. Unfortunately, when I enquired the course was full so I put that idea on hold. I considered various other options but perhaps I started to realise that I had no great career ambition myself. As I got older, I started to find big changes seemed more daunting than exciting. I think if money had been an issue then that would have made a huge difference, but fortunately, for us that was not the case at all.

Eventually after a time I did manage to secure a very nice position in a Building Society, telling myself that however daunting this may seem I could do it. I remained part- time but with slightly more hours than I had done before. It was similar to the bank in some ways but also quite different in others. Very soon, I found I was actually really enjoying it, finding it both satisfying and interesting and, importantly, still with lots of contact with different people.

The world of banking had been a revelation for me. I hadn't been aware of such a scale of opportunities and progression available. I learned also that my preconception that it would all be above my head was totally misplaced and ridiculous. I could do this and moreover I was doing it and, if I may say so, quite well too.

The team I worked with were super and as with any job, this does make a big difference. Our manager was excellent and the fun and banter within the team was the best I had ever experienced, even than in the bank. I soon became aware that I was very happy indeed in my new job; it had provided a change of scene and some new challenges and I felt much better in myself.

I remembered all the friends and colleagues in the past constantly moaning about the drudgery of being bored or suffering a meaningless job, or bitching about someone at work daily. I had none of this here, in fact far from it.

Paul and I had made a lovely circle of friends both at work and at home over the years. There is 'the gang', a large group of fourteen who we see as regularly as a crowd of such size can coordinate their diary. We also became friends with many couples, all of whom we see from time to time, but some more than others do.

I won't list them all, but I will mention first and foremost, Paul and Gloria. They were the first couple I got to know quite well (through Paul as the boys worked together). We had met just before I finally here moved down to Dorset, when I would come down from Barrow for the weekend. Now we live quite close and see them regularly. I've become incredibly fond of them both over the years. We enjoy socialising with them both at home, or away as we did on a few occasions holiday together.

Then there are Julie and Mick. They moved into a house around the corner from us with their lovely children Michaela and Ian. I first came to know Julie as we worked together in the bank. We see them regularly too. They love walking and camping and have accumulated a wide range of (mostly huge) tents and we try to join them on a camping weekend during the summer months. Waking up to Mick's legendary barbecued breakfasts is a real treat.

Jo and Chris, both of whom worked with Paul, live in a lovely house in Wiltshire. We would see them socially but not quite so often due to the distance. They are a lovely couple; very easy going and most certainly knew how to throw a super party in their beautiful garden with delightful countryside views; a perfect setting for many a splendid barbecue. We were very lucky to have a great set of friends and a good social calendar we always enjoyed their company.

Then there was Mark and Jo, who we came to know quite a bit later. He worked for the same company as Paul. They had one son, Tom, and their daughter Ellen was born as I got to know them a little more and it was then really that we all became friends. We saw them less than some of our other friends as they had young children and lived out of town, but they also had a particular close set of fiends who they saw regularly as they lived almost on each other's doorstep. Mark, in particular, was very easy going and fun whenever we all got on well together. We enjoyed each other's company; we would talk, dance, and sing late into the night, with Mark often playing his guitar and us singing along.

# CHAPTER THIRTY-FOUR

Paul had actually taken a role working away a number of days a week and he would stay away a night or two. He would come back home in the middle of the week and work locally and the following Monday he would set off for work again. For a while, it was a rather nice, almost welcome change really. I only had myself to see to and the housework took no time with only me at home to mess it up.

I had been without him in Barrow years ago of course when he'd first started to work down in Dorchester from Monday to Friday. I didn't like it but it was only temporary and we had a wonderful future to look forward to in the South, so we'd coped and our life now proved it had all been worth it. Back then, though, I'd had Sarah-Jane at home.

It was strange at first but I soon got used to it and once again found my routine. I am far from obsessive but I do like to get into a routine with my housework and jobs and like to consider myself a rather organised person. I really cannot bear mess and disorganisation; I think this also stems from Paul being so tidy-minded and organised, very much an important part of his job as a planning engineer, but he, too, liked the place neat and tidy.

Our Silver Wedding was going to be in a few years and I gave this some considerable thought as to how we could celebrate it. Then it struck me that there would be no better place to do this but Australia, a place I have longed and dreamed to visit. When Paul next came home, I suggested it to him.

"Gosh! Well that's going to be expensive but you've given me nearly four years of warning! I'll think about it; just leave it to me and I will prepare and save and we will have the money sorted by then." I shrieked with delight and already was getting excited about it, as there would be lots to plan. We needed to decide what we want to see and do there and of course what time of year to go. I couldn't believe it – I was going to Oz!

I was also becoming aware of a welcome but pleasant change in my husband. He seemed happier and rather more 'laid back' than of late. He didn't seem to be quite so short tempered and was a bit more amiable. We'd got into a good routine quite quickly with his working away and had adapted to our 'different life.' He was clearly very happy in his new job and I knew how important that was I for him too, as he hadn't seemed happy or settled at work for some time really, not so far as I was concerned anyway.

The next few years passed; Paul was in the same job, as was I. We had a holiday each year, including going to Florida where we stayed at Lake Buena vista. We had an *amazing* time there, doing all those 'must-do' theme Parks. Unusually, perhaps, my favourite was Sea World. I loved feeding the dolphins, but, despite much encouragement, I could not be persuaded to get into the water with them – that was a step too far for me I'm afraid. I could also have gone on an escorted voyage with a Beluga Whale, but again, that was a definite no from me. I was particularly thrilled with Shamu, the Killer Whale; it was incredible, seeing humans swimming with them, even in Shamu's mouth! It was simply astounding.

It was here, though, that a lone polar bear took my breath away; and a little of my heart, too. He was in a reasonable sized enclosure with toys and other things around him, but he lay still and all alone. I don't know why but that really upset me. As I looked at him, I began to cry.

I found myself going back to the window to see him repeatedly to see if he had moved, but he hadn't. He was just lying perfectly still on a cold slab. I hoped he was sleeping. We eventually finished the visit when I'd managed to drag myself away from the window, and made our way back to the hotel. We prepared to go out on the bus along International Drive that evening to take in more of the area and find a nice place to eat, which in Florida isn't hard or expensive to do at all. We had a lovely evening and a super meal (huge portions!) before making our way home again. Both of us were feeling very tired after another busy day.

The following morning, we woke refreshed and ready for the day ahead. We discussed at breakfast the plan for the day which was to include some shopping and a bit of sun worshipping (for me anyway as Paul didn't really enjoy it). Since yesterday, however, I'd found myself constantly thinking about the polar bear. I just couldn't get him out of my mind and it made be so sad, so I asked if we could pop back in just to see him once more. Paul didn't mind really, as the bus stopped right outside our hotel at regular intervals so off we went. I was glad to be going but also a little doubtful as it really had quite affected me.

I headed straight for the Arctic area where he'd been yesterday, stopping briefly on the way to stroke a stingray in the huge tank. I laughed as we passed the penguins waddling as we got nearer the to the Polar Bear enclosure. I walked up to the glass and I couldn't see him; my heart sank and I could feel the tears beginning to sting my eyes once more. I felt such a fool but I just couldn't help the effect this magnificent but seemingly lonely bear had on me.

Suddenly at the back of his den from behind a wall he appeared. I immediately stopped crying and was now smiling like the Cheshire cat. I couldn't have dreamt for what happened next: he walked right up to the front of the enclosure and put his great paw on the glass almost in a 'high five' gesture. I reached and placed my hand over it my side of the glass and he looked straight down at me.

I was crying once more but this time they were tears of great joy. I was in a trance momentarily, and then I started talking to him. I removed my hand and just stood in awe watching him for what seemed an eternity. I was now extremely happy and after a while decided to drag myself away, I said goodbye (yes, I know I'm bonkers, but I can't help it) and walked away. As I did so, he began to play with one of his toys. I left, feeling exhilarated, having had a chance encounter, another that I shall never forget.

# CHAPTER THIRTY-FIVE

We were about eighteen months away from our Silver Wedding Anniversary and I had been thinking a great deal about Australia and what we might like to do while we were there. Paul hadn't mentioned it for some time but I thought we should start thinking about booking the flights soon, if he hadn't already done so, although I doubted that was likely.

I gently broached the subject, as I didn't want to rain on his parade in case he was quietly sorting it out, and had it already planned as a surprise. It really would have been a surprise if he'd done that he had never yet booked a holiday! But then there's a first time for everything, I remembered, that he'd said "leave it to me" when I'd first suggested the idea and so I'd done just that.

"Can I just ask how the Australia funds are coming on and whether you've any ideas on dates? It's only 18 months away until our anniversary." The reply was brief and not at all what I was hoping to hear.

"Oh, you can forget that! There is *no* way we will be going to Australia. I haven't done anything about it. There's simply no way we can afford to go next year so you'll have to forget the idea I'm afraid!"

I couldn't believe my ears. Why had he not done as he promised almost three years before? More importantly, why had he not told me of this before now, especially when he knew how much I wanted it? I was amazed by his reaction but, more than anything, I felt so let down.

I stayed silent for a while, trying to take it all in, before asking him why and what had happened.

"I just haven't done anything about it, alright and now we are out of time. Maybe in another five or six years." Once he'd spoken, I knew that was the end of it. I didn't bother saying anything else. It wasn't worth it; there was no point. I was going to get nowhere banging on about it when he'd clearly made up his mind, so the subject was closed – indefinitely.

Much later, just a few months before our anniversary date and most unexpectedly, he presented me with a lovely eternity ring. He did in front of all his work colleagues, which was a lovely surprise and very romantic. It was a beautiful ring and such a wonderful gesture, especially as he rarely did anything very romantic. Nonetheless, it was not Australia.

Over the coming weeks, I thought more about our silver anniversary and consoled myself with the thought that we would still be able to do something nice by way of celebration. I was determined that we would so put on my thinking cap! I wanted to do something special – our twenty-five years of marriage more than warranted it. I thought of maybe a romantic cruise or a week somewhere in Europe, but as he doesn't really like the sun, I thought that would seem more for me and I wanted to do something for us both.

Suddenly it hit me! Why don't we renew our vows in church? As we were married in Barrow, I immediately thought about that church, St Mary's, or maybe our local Dorchester church, St George's, followed by a party for everyone somewhere nearby. What a fabulous idea, I thought. I was on the case now and very excited about the prospect. In no time, I'd made a number of enquiries with the vicars in Barrow and Dorchester, and had visited and made enquiries with few venues I felt suitable for the party. There couldn't be too many guests and I thought best to keep it down to a modest guest list. The more I thought about the logistics of going to Barrow, however, the more I decided that it wasn't practical, so I reluctantly discounted that option.

St Georges in Dorchester is a lovely church, quite large, but a very good alternative. Sarah went frequently and helped with the crèche there on a Sunday. She had also been confirmed there, and Paul and I attended occasionally after we married. It felt a most appropriate choice indeed.

I considered what we would wear and as our anniversary is in September, I thought autumnal colours would be the perfect choice. I then tackled the tricky question of whether I would do it as a surprise for Paul. I'd previously arranged a surprise fortieth birthday party for him; it was a huge success and he was both pleased and touched with all the thought I'd put into it. Our silver anniversary celebration I thought was likely to be much more expensive and as Paul holds the purse strings, I felt it much the best option to discuss and arrange the final details with him.

One Saturday on a quiet weekend, I decided to tell him my idea. I was very excited and carefully picked my moment during the early evening. I reminded him that our silver wedding wasn't too far away by then and said that I'd understood his decision about Australia (I most certainly didn't, but thought it best to leave it there).

"I think it would be nice to do something special to celebrate, so what about renewing our vows in church and then having a party or dinner somewhere with our friends and family?"

He looked at me in complete horror.

"You must be joking!" he spat. "If you think I'm going to pay for that you can think again, no way!" I stood still and in complete silence for what seemed an age, numbed by his hurtful reaction. I stared at him in complete disbelief.

"What a horrid response! How could you be so cold? Why does everything have to come down to money with you? I thought it was a wonderful, romantic idea and a most special and memorable way to spend our twenty-fifth wedding anniversary. I have put a lot of thought and time into this and for what? A miserable, heartless and miserly reply, that's what! I really don't know why I bother!"

I left the room and went up to our bedroom, fell onto the bed and cried into the pillow. I was churning over his response in mind; all I could see was his miserable, angry expression and hear his stinging, nasty words. He didn't even come up to see me. Well one thing was for sure: I knew exactly where I stood on this now, and I wasn't going to mention the dreaded day again. I pulled myself together, showered again and headed back down to the lounge. Paul knew I was angry and avoided the subject completely. Instead, he brought me a glass of wine and changed the subject. I was still reeling but played along. I retired to bed after watching some crappy film, Paul following immediately at my heels.

The subject wasn't broached again for some time. I wasn't going to mention it. He eventually suggested, however, that we should have a party to celebrate our big occasion. He felt we ought to do something so said he would make enquiries about hiring a room at various venues. He insisted that we could do the catering ourselves – there were to be no outside caterers, as we had to keep the cost to a minimum.

So that was it; our silver wedding anniversary. I spent the whole day, with help from Paul, Sarah and Mark, doing all the catering and dressing the room in the local Corn Exchange function room. We worked from nine-thirty that morning to four-thirty in the afternoon. By the time we got back home to get ready for the evening and back to the hall I was so tired and could hardly be bothered to face the evening. I put on a brave face and welcomed our guests as they arrived, it wasn't anything big or special at all. Afterwards we stayed late to clear everything away and leave the room as we had found it, as was expected. It went very well and our guests had a good time, but I didn't really enjoy it; it was such hard work and not at all how I'd dreamt of celebrating this milestone event.

# CHAPTER THIRTY-SIX

Some of the next few chapters I find myself writing were without doubt the hardest of all to put onto paper. I am going to be as careful as I can in describing what happened and the difficulties encountered.

Having someone dip in and out of your daily life for any length of time means you have to adjust and adapt to a new way of life; from the simplest tasks like changing a light bulb or disposing of a spider to when, how and what you eat or what to watch on television. I've always been a convivial person who enjoys company and being alone so much was an adjustment, that was fine from time-to-time but not for prolonged periods. While Paul was away with work we spoke daily on the phone for quarter of an hour or so to catch up, but sadly that was about it.

I missed him very much indeed and found myself wishing the week or days away until he would come home so we could enjoy the weekend together and maybe catch up with family and friends. Suddenly the weekend would be over and he was once again leaving for another spell away. I know that lots of people live like this and some are gone for weeks or even months, but this was not a premise I liked very much. It wasn't how life should be. You don't marry to be with the person you love to spend half your life apart. As I've said before money was not an issue at all for us, despite Paul's sometimes overly-careful approach to it, so I began to wonder why we were doing this.

He was working on the Isle of Wight and I began to go there for weekends or the odd night here and there, at Paul's suggestion. To begin with, at least it was fun as I had never been before; although quite a small island it is very pretty, certainly in the summer and it, at first, made a most welcome change. I began to look forward to going over; he used to meet me off the ferry and take me to the hotel where we would change before trying one of the local restaurants and pubs.

During the days, while he was at work I would explore the island. One day I walked to the impressive Osborne House in East Cowes, Queen Victoria's former holiday residence. On other occasions, I'd walk to Gurnard to ramble among the streets and explore the shops. I went to the island a number of times and soon I think I'd walked the length and breadth of the island. It was always very welcoming and I felt quite at home there, so much so I did at one point browse a few estate agents' websites, looking at properties for sale. I came and went over to the island and Paul came and went back home and it was nice for a time.

He came home one day after working in Christchurch; we were talking as usual about the day when I suddenly realised that he seemed different; unresponsive and rather less chatty than normal. I left it a while and later decided I ought to ask if he was OK. He said he was fine, so I didn't push it anymore; if he wanted to talk about it he no doubt would.

As the end of the week came, we were looking forward to a nice weekend together at home, nothing special, but nicely chilled and relaxed. On the Saturday we'd seen some friends who lived close by; in fact we'd gone to them for a lovely meal, but Paul had seemed rather antagonistic towards her as well as twitchy to get home. We left and walked back in the rain. He'd made me feel more than a little uncomfortable in front of our friends and I said so. We ended up 'having words' while we were still walking and Paul ended up once more in one of his interminable 'sulks'.

Sunday came and went in virtual silence. It was awful, I hated the atmosphere and it was not lost on me that over time Paul's moods were becoming more and more frequent. Piecing various things together, I thought it was something to do with his work, or with someone at work, perhaps his boss. I even told him I thought that was the problem and suggested that he needed to do something to rectify the situation as it was becoming increasingly wearing and worrying.

Monday morning came and he went off again. Rather than missing him, this time I almost felt a sense of relief when he left. It was then that I started to realise things maybe weren't as they should be. The realisation that I felt more relaxed and at ease when he was away hit me like a brick. I could watch what I wanted on the television that evening without being told to, "Turn that rubbish off!" or, "You aren't watching that are you?" and, "Why have you got that rubbish on?" He would always get his way.

If I was engrossed in a book, as I like to do from time to time, he hated it; he would huff and say, "I may as well not be here" or, "Haven't you finished that yet?" So inevitably I'd put the book down until I could read it when he was away or out of the house.

The more I thought about things, the more warning signs I noticed. He hadn't told me that I'd looked nice since I couldn't remember when. If I asked him for a bit of reassurance with a "Do I look OK?" question he'd tell me I was being an attention-seeker and that I knew I looked fine so why was I asking. This made me feel awkward and silly with my own husband; having a compliment paid on occasion is nice and he'd always done so in the past. The warm-hearted man I knew had become cold and distant.

There is an old saying that no-one knows what goes on behind closed doors. I, too, am not perfect I know, neither do I want to write pages and pages about the problems and issues that were becoming increasingly obvious to me by now. However, I do want to give a true view or some sense of how things had become before continuing further with this book as our problems were contributory factors in the final outcome.

So let me just say that things now were starting to build up. I felt uneasy and more than a little concerned, but what upset me most were the long, moody and deafening silences, it seemed, too, with his harsh and unkind words, this was bound to have a huge detrimental impact on us as a couple.

The next three days flew by as I busied myself. I had done a bit of painting in the dining room. We'd recently bought a new dining table and matching sideboard and I wanted to spruce the room up a little. I'd started by just touching up a few marks with some paint we had left over from when we'd original decorated the room, but I ended up painting almost the whole room. I do tend to get carried away as I enjoy painting and find it rather therapeutic. I had bought a pair of new curtains in the local department store on the way home from work; they were in the sale, reduced to £20 from £110 (I do love a bargain!). I was so pleased with them; once I had pressed and hung them they looked fabulous, the room seemed transformed and very fresh it looked really lovely.

I felt so happy. It had kept me busy doing something that I liked and I'd gained a great sense of pleasure and satisfaction when I'd finished, and after all, I am here seven days a week. Paul never did much decorating, he never did enjoy it, then not everyone does, and when he did he was so slap dash and messy about it. He once painted the wall in the lounge around the TV without even pulling it out! I noticed sometime later when we bought a new television and the shape of the old one was like a mural on the wall. Nor did he see the utility in dustsheets so I'd frequently end up having to clean paint splashes from the carpet and furniture. As a result, decorating was now mostly my domain, but I didn't mind at all, as I do enjoy it.

Before I knew, it was Wednesday. I put a nice meal in the oven and for a change decided to walk to the station to meet him off the train. He seemed very surprised to see me, but pleased.

We went home hand in hand and I put his dirty clothes in to wash. Before I'd left the house, I had pre-set the table in the newly decorated dining room and closed the door on it. I was going to wait to show him the room until I'd called him down from the lounge (it was a three-storey mews house with living area on the middle floor) to come and eat. He came in and sat down at the table. I saw him look at the curtains, but he didn't say anything, nothing at all, which was most unlike him.

During the meal, we talked, but still no comment about the curtains or the room. After the meal, I took out the dishes and decided I would ask his opinion.

"Yes of course I noticed them," he snapped, "but what was wrong with the other ones?" His mouth was set stiffly, a now familiar sign of displeasure.

"There was nothing wrong with them," I replied, "but these match beautifully, I paid for them with my money and they were only £20! What's the problem? Don't you like them?"

"It's not I don't like them," he retorted. "It's just silly! You need something better to do with your time, Sue!" I was deflated and the moment was ruined. I said I would take them down and return them the next day, as I'd kept the receipt and packaging. I knew I'd caved in, but I didn't want an atmosphere, not again.

The tone was now set for the evening, so I cleared everything away, filled the dishwasher and tidied the kitchen whilst he went to watch *The Simpsons*. I could hear him laughing, so hoped his mood might have lightened by the time I went back upstairs.

Once I'd finished I opened a bottle of red wine and poured him a glass and, as I don't like red wine, I poured myself a glass of white and took them up. I handed Paul his wine; he looked at me witheringly and shook his head.

"We don't need wine, Sue. Take it down and put it back in the bottle." I felt like telling him I wanted mine and would pour his back, but I decided it just wasn't worth the hassle so I obeyed and poured them both back. I was annoyed, upset and felt small. Why does he have to be so controlling I thought to myself? I went down to the study where I played solitaire on the computer and surfed holiday sites whilst listening to Westlife.

An hour or so later I went up to tell him I was off to bed and see if was coming. He said he was watching *New Tricks* and would come up once it had finished. We'd always gone to bed together, but him following me later had crept in, too, of late, I'd noticed.

On Thursday, he was working in Christchurch and left quite early to go with a friend as they were sharing the driving. I got up, did my jobs, and went into the dining room to take down the curtains. I felt so disappointed and as they did look so nice I made the decision they were staying up, and I didn't care what he said. I'd bought and paid for them with my own money so they were not going back. My heart was pounding as I wondered what the repercussions were going to be but I was determined I wasn't going to let him override me this time.

I showered and set off for work. I loved my job and always looked forwards to going in in the morning. I had a very good morning, I'd already exceeded my weekly target of appointments and bookings, so received plenty of praise from my boss and colleagues. I went home at 1 p.m. feeling very pleased with my achievements but started to worry about the curtains as soon as I saw the house on my approach. I collected the steps from the garage on the way in, went straight through to the dining room and began to take the curtains down. I folded them carefully and put them back in the bag with the receipt.

I was hungry by that time and I don't cope with being hungry, and when coupled with tiredness less so. I quickly changed out of my uniform, prepared my lunch and took it into the freshly painted dining room where I sat at our lovely new dining table. I stared at the bare windows. I took one bite of my cheese and onion sandwich and burst into tears. I was sobbing, with my head in my hands and tears dripping onto our new ash dining table making dark splotches as they fell. I pushed my barely touched sandwich to one side as I was no longer hungry, took a sip of my tea pulled myself together and just sat quietly thinking.

What is happening here? What is wrong with him? He had turned into a Jekyll and Hyde character of late and I hated it. I always looked to blame myself at such times; that was the easy option: clear the air and move on to avoid the conflict and the moods. Not this time. I was determined I wouldn't do it. Every time I blamed myself, it was simply an escape for him, as it put me in the wrong and made him look faultless. In my eyes Paul used to be faultless, but I was seeing a different man now, one who often felt a stranger.

I went into the kitchen, threw away my untouched sandwich and went back into the dining room. I picked out a Pet Shop Boys CD, put it on, turned the volume up and took the curtains back out of the bag to re-hang them. I felt a little uneasy doing it, but the music was keeping me focused. I was singing along and even breaking into the occasional dance. There's nothing like music to raise my spirits.

By the end of the second track, I was feeling better again and I continued with my housework whilst singing and dancing to the beat of Phil Collins' *Dancing to the Light* CD. Washing all done, dried and ironed. Rooms dusted, hoovered and all the windows on the ground floor cleaned, grass cut and borders tended. I was feeling so much better and I would deal with any repercussions should there be any when he came home. I still felt a little uneasy – I don't like conflict but my mind was made up.

Paul came home later that day and things were OK. The curtains had been forgotten and we got through the weekend without any issues. Bless him, he was tired; working, travelling and living between two places must catch up with you.

Monday morning came again so fast and off he went again.

This period of unease had gone on for months. Or was it years? I wanted to know what the reasons were behind it all. I'd asked numerous times for reassurance, whether he had any worries about anything but I always got the same sharp reply. "I'm fine." I felt uneasy and unsettled. A few friends had even asked if everything was OK between us, or were concerned as Paul didn't seem himself. I'd brush it away as tiredness. I didn't want people to know or think there were problems and bother them with it. Or perhaps I didn't want to admit it to myself.

We started to go away to hotels for the occasional weekend break, which made a lovely change for me. For Paul, however, it was something of a 'busman's holiday' as he spent so much time away in hotels with work. He did, I think, sometimes enjoy it.

However, the moods and the atmosphere were always there, not far away. I began to ask myself again whether it was me after all, maybe something I had said or done. I just couldn't see, though, how this was all down to me. It takes two to have an argument as they say, and I know no one is perfect. Nevertheless, I was also starting to think that maybe my parents perhaps years ago had possibly been right after all about Paul changing me. Perhaps I shall never really know.

# CHAPTER THIRTY-SEVEN

I don't know why, but Paul never answered the phone at home, except for the regular Sunday call from his mother. We were in the kitchen one Saturday morning before flying out to Spain that afternoon to spend a week in Barcelona, another bargain I'd found, when the phone rang. I was cooking a full English breakfast at the time; we had our friends Jo and Chris with us who'd stayed with us overnight after we'd all been out to a function the previous evening.

As usual, I answered it while Paul just looked at me whilst turning the bacon, waiting for me to take it. I heard a voice that I recognised after a few moments: it was Mark, Sarah-Jane's boyfriend. He was full of cold, which is why his voice sounded unfamiliar at first.

"Hi, Sue. How are you?" He asked politely. I said we were all good and he asked to speak to Paul. I passed him the phone. They spoke only very briefly over the noise of the bacon hissing and sausages sizzling I heard Paul say

"Well yes, of course. Oh and good luck!"

With a puzzled expression on my face, I asked Paul what that had been about. He turned to me, beaming, as he put the phone down.

"Gosh!" he said, now looking a bit shocked. "It was Mark! He rang to ask for my permission for Sarah's hand in marriage!"

Well you could have knocked me down with a feather. I yelped with joy and before I knew it, Jo and I were hugging jumping up and down screaming with sheer delight in the kitchen. I was beside myself with happiness. I had thought about this from time to time and wondered to Paul whether they might get married. I'd thought that we ought to perhaps prepare ourselves, as they had been courting for quite some time. It was truly wonderful news and despite my musings, it was a complete surprise.

Jo and Chris left after breakfast. I hadn't been hungry anymore I was simply too excited to eat. I could think of nothing else at all; I was on a complete high. Paul and I left for the airport and Sarah rang me whilst we were on our way to tell us her exciting news. She was crying with joy, so much so that she could barely get the words out, I told her to hang up and ring me back when she'd calmed down, but she composed herself and told me everything.

They were in Wales at the time, staying in a lovely guesthouse in Snowdonia (this much we'd known). They had climbed Mount Snowdon and reached the summit and started what seemed was a snowball fight. Mark reached for what Sarah thought was another snowball when in fact he was removing the beautiful diamond ring that he packed so carefully inside his rucksack. How romantic!

Of course Sarah accepted and they'd soon set a date for 2nd October 2010, some two years away. I was so happy and very delighted for them both. Whilst on holiday I took every opportunity to drop it into conversation with total strangers. I didn't care! I wanted the world to know! This was a mother's prerogative and one of the many reasons I'd always wanted a daughter; so we could enjoy the white wedding and all that goes with it, planning everything from venues to hen do's to wedding dresses and hats. I knew by now that was what she wanted. I simply couldn't wait for that day; I wanted her to have the wedding she so rightfully deserved. I was a very proud Mother of a beautiful daughter who I knew was going to make the most beautiful bride indeed for Mark.

# CHAPTER THIRTY-EIGHT

Christmas that year came and went and was very enjoyable. Paul's Mum had come down as was usual and we had a nice dinner before opening our presents. My main one from Paul was a baby pink fluffy dressing gown from M&S; it was *exactly* the same as the one he'd bought me the previous Christmas. He apologised for the repetition, but said he couldn't think of what else to buy me! Paul was delighted with the watch I'd bought him. It wasn't a designer watch – he often said he wouldn't thank me for one as expensive watches were for poseurs. As long as you can tell the time, that was all that mattered.

We would always spread the present-opening throughout the day to make them last. On Christmas evening we'd usually saved one present to open, along with a nice bottle of wine and some chocolates, listening to the music on the CD I had usually received from him or someone else that day.

This Christmas we had something else to think about. In fact, all my days and nights were now filled with "The Wedding": the church; the reception venue; Sarah's dress; the guest list. Then there were the dress and hat for the mother-of-the bride (Paul had, of course, budgeted an amount I was allowed to spend). I had been assured by the bride-to-be that I would be allowed to wear the biggest hat of all! Me and dressing up: that has always gone together like Posh & Becks or Scarlett O'Hara & Rhett Butler! I just love to dress up, and what better excuse does a mother need than this!

I was so *unbelievably* excited. Paul however, remained his typical unemotional self about the whole thing. I was quite surprised though; this was to be his day-of-days too, the day he proudly walked his daughter up the aisle to hand her to such a lovely man, who had proved his worth in the manner of the engagement. It doesn't really get much better or more satisfying, does it?

Dad, or 'Bank of Dad' as he had self-appointed himself, was on the case now with the financial side of things. His ultimate and favourite domain: the money. Sarah had been firing off emails, messages and phone calls about all things wedding: likes and dislikes; desires and dreads; do's and don'ts. The Bank of Dad's spreadsheet was growing and growing and the financial implications were being accounted for to the penny. It may sound harsh, but sadly true and he didn't like it, not one little bit.

He would disappear for hours into the study (or the 'counting house' as I'd quietly re-named it) before coming up for air some time later, scratching his head. I could always tell immediately by his face when it wasn't going to be good; over the years I'd come to recognise every look, expression and tone – and exactly what they all meant.

"This bloody wedding list is growing and growing" he'd exclaim. "It's ridiculous … Sue, it's getting quite out of control." He always had a good head of hair but imagined him bald come the day at this pace.

His main bone of contention was with the guest list, or more to the point, Mark's side of it. It dwarfed the Barker side!

"We're going to have to say something, Sue!" he went on.

"It's hardly Mark's fault we have virtually no family left" I'd explain. "We're already bulking our side up with our friends."

We had initially set aside a certain budget but inevitably the cost was growing. Mark's parents had very kindly offered to pay a quarter of the total cost and that was a great help, or so I'd thought. Even that was wrong though. He thought it a rather tight offering from them. I tried to help by introducing some levity.

"Well, fortunately we'll only have it to do once! Anyway, we should be thankful, and pride ourselves in giving her a day she will remember. She deserves it."

My words didn't help at all and I stood accused of being silly about it and encouraging her extravagance. We were going to be visiting her soon; she knew none of the financial aggravation it was causing at home and neither did I want her to. As I'd done so often in the past, like during her university days, I tried to calm the waters and plead with him not to say anything to upset it.

It was just after Christmas when we went to Sarah and Mark's and I'd talked to Paul before we left home to make sure we kept it all calm. I knew he was going to kick off, I could read him like a book.

They lived together in their lovely flat in Farnborough. We arrived and Grandma was with us. Sarah was on her own as Mark (who is a policeman) was at work on a day shift. We went inside and had a cup of tea and naturally, the subject of the wedding was soon broached. My heart was pounding, as I just knew there was going to be a disagreement. I'd been there many times and today the vibes weren't good.

"Anyway, Sarah, about the guest list!" he revved up. Here we go, I thought. I shan't go into the details of his rant, but it's fair to say that he put his points across most firmly on a number of things. Even in my darker moments, I hadn't quite expected his curt bluntness. He was virtually shouting at her, displaying his immense displeasure. Sadly, neither did Sarah-Jane expect it, nor his mother. Within minutes Sarah-Jane was in pieces, breaking her heart, sobbing in the kitchen.

I'd always tried to be peacemaker; after all, I'm the one who had to live with him when we got back home. Even I was finding it hard this time, as I didn't agree with any of his issues. If he'd had his way, Paul would rather have given them a cheque towards a deposit on a house; he didn't see it as our job to pay for the whole wedding, it should be just a contribution.

He really thought they ought to pay for the bulk themselves:

"They're living together – have been for some time – and they're both earning a good salary with good jobs." I still felt it was the bride's parents' responsibility. Maybe I was wrong (and I do admit I can be on occasion) but I didn't think so now.

Mother came into the kitchen then and quietly asked what on earth had got into Paul. She couldn't understand it.

"Me neither, Ma, but this is what he's like and has been for a while, I'm afraid," I tried to explain. He did have good moments and he was lovely then but "I'm sorry to say he really has crossed the line this time."

We went back into the lounge with Sarah. Through her tears she pointed at the door and told her father to leave.

"I don't want you in my house, Dad. Will you please leave now!" I didn't blame her at all.

I felt so sorry for her and was fighting back my own tears. I wasn't going to give in.

"Are you happy now?" I asked. "Just look what you've done to her, coming into her home and reducing her to tears over her wedding. I really don't know what's wrong with you, Paul. You have done a perfect job of ruining Sarah's day ... and mine!" His mother sat there stunned, seeing another side to her son, a side I imagine she didn't like either.

Eventually I managed to calm Sarah down. She clearly didn't want to talk to Paul who was still in the flat, behaving as if he'd done nothing wrong at all. I decided that we ought to leave and respect her wishes, as there was no sign of him letting up on the subject whatsoever. We left and made our way back to Dorchester in two hours of silence.

There was nothing more I could do. I had no intention of raising it again and had made my feelings and opinion perfectly clear on the subject; he knew I was far from happy, but that didn't seem to matter. The wedding for him had become a taboo subject and I wasn't going to stand for it anymore. I had had enough of his ridiculous behaviour and was going to put my foot down firmly once and for all. I was determined my daughter was going to have the day she wanted and that was the end of it. This whole sorry episode was further proof, if any were needed, that things really were far from right with Paul.

When we eventually spoke again I was still *so* angry at him but managed to hold it back. I once again asked if there was anything else bothering him. As usual, he insisted there wasn't. I was so unhappy and really worried about Paul and what was wrong with him. For so, so long I'd had to put up with his mood swings. There were still some days when he was fine and 'normal' relations could be resumed but his "Mr Hyde" side was increasingly coming to the fore.

I thought he needed to see the doctor but I absolutely knew he wouldn't go, so that would have been a pointless suggestion. I was starting to think he was either ill or possibly going through some form midlife crisis as he was by now in his late forties. I loved him very much but couldn't stop worrying about our future and us. I was far from happy and however much I loved him he had become a changed man these last few years, something that had become very noticeable to others.

After the visit to Sarah, things did improve a little and we went away for a weekend to a lovely hotel near Henley-on-Thames. Whilst we were there relaxing in the Jacuzzi together, he broached the subject of our fiftieth birthdays, which were just over a year away and only a week apart. I was certainly surprised, but very pleased and listened to his suggestions. I have to say that, given my disappointments over our Silver Wedding and Australia trip I was finding it hard to show any great interest or enthusiasm. I joined in the conversation, albeit half-heartedly. One ground-rule I did lay down was that I was *not* going to do the catering, but after surprising Paul for his fortieth birthday party, I thought I'd leave him to sort this one. Let's see what happens.

# CHAPTER THIRTY-NINE

We had been invited for a meal to our friends Mark and Jo for an evening meal and overnight stay. We hadn't seen them for a little while there was lots of news to share and plenty to talk about.

We had a few drinks before dinner was served in the conservatory, a lovely acquisition erected only a few years previously. We ate heartily before retiring to the lounge, listening to music with a bit of singing and dancing before Mark as usual picked up his guitar and started to play requests. He can be a little shy, but does love to play and he's pretty good at it, too.

Mark and I were sat together talking and I asked him why he was so modest about his obvious talent and ability on the guitar. Completely unexpectedly, he turned to look at me and whispered to me.

"Sue, I am so in love with you and have been for quite some time now. I just don't know what to do about it." Mouth open in disbelief, I was sure I must have misheard him, but no, he repeated it word-for-word. I *had* heard him quite clearly first time.

To say I was stunned would be a huge understatement. I was silent – that doesn't happen very often. I turned back to him:

"Oh, Mark, don't say that! Please Don't!"

Still talking under his voice he went on: "I'm sorry, Sue, but it's true. I need to talk to you about it; I'm going out of my mind."

"I don't want to talk about it and now I want to go to bed." I tried to brush it off and put it down to the alcohol as plenty had been consumed. I looked across at Paul and Jo who were happily oblivious to this, lost in conversation. I didn't know what to do but I stood up and excused myself.

"I'm tired and going up to bed, it's rather late." Paul soon followed and he too was merry, we all were. At least I had been, but now I felt suddenly very sober.

Needless to say, I didn't sleep at all. I tossed and turned, cried and tried to clear my mind, but I just couldn't get the words out of my head. I could see his face as clearly as if here were still sat in front of me. What if he really meant it?

I had to admit I liked him. I liked him very much. We had always got on really well, as I had done with all our friends, although I did always feel different with him; he always seemed so sincere, genuine and 'together'. We talked about anything and everything and always seemed to enjoy our conversation whatever it happened to be. He always seemed interested in me, listening intently to whatever I had to say, and quite often helpful and useful advice he'd give. We also laughed and laughed when we were together, but then these are all signs of a good friendship, aren't they?

Morning came and I decided to just ignore what had been said when I saw him, still blaming the alcohol. Then we would go home and all would be forgotten. I came down the stairs to see him stood looking up at me, wearing a terribly sad, meaningful expression; I brushed past him and went into the kitchen where Paul and Jo were talking.

We left soon after breakfast and I worried all the way home as to how I was going tell Paul; I had to say something, but I couldn't come up with any easy answer. Maybe the answer was just avoiding contact with them and it would all just fade away. I decided I would think about it when my head was clear and after I'd slept as I'd had precious little sleep that night.

We arrived home and I went to bed straight away. I was exhausted and desperately needed sleep; I am not at my best when I am tired and I had so much to think about: what was I to do with the situation I now found myself in? I needed to be alert and firing on all cylinders to talk to Paul about it. I tossed and turned for ages worrying about it, but thankfully, I did eventually drift off.

More than two hours later, I woke refreshed and needing a cup of tea; I suddenly remembered Mark's big announcement the night before. I started to feel sick now with nerves. What was Mark thinking? Coming out with such words, it's ridiculous. He's a married man with two children. I am a married woman with a daughter who incidentally is getting married. How could he do this?

I got out of bed and into the shower. My mind was full of his words; I could see his face clearly, as he'd spoken them, his eyes so meaningful. Oh what has he done? Suddenly I was trembling and then began to cry. I was so taken aback. I had to tell Paul so decided to go downstairs, sit down and simply tell him the truth.

I was getting dressed and Paul came up to the room.

"I thought I heard the shower. I wondered if you were going to get up at all today," he said. "I've cut the grass and started a bit of gardening. What are we having for lunch?" Lunch? I couldn't possibly eat anything!

"I don't know, Paul, something easy" I said. "What do you fancy? Are you very hungry? I'll come down and have a look in a minute and make you something."

I made the bed, went down, and looked out of the first floor window and he was back in the garden. I watched him for a moment and began to tremble. I started to feel nauseous again and my heart sank. I was welling up once more, but I couldn't cry, not now. I went into the bathroom and splashed my face with cold water before heading down to the kitchen. In the fridge, I found some cooked meat and cheese and thought with crusty bread that would do fine for lunch. Not that I was hungry; I wanted, nothing at all. It wasn't a great offering for Sunday lunchtime but I knew I just couldn't make a roast dinner, not today.

I went into the garden and suggested my lunch idea and he said it would be fine. He looked tired himself. I don't know if he'd slept while I'd gone back to bed, but he seemed happily busy so I left him to it. I went indoors and prepared lunch, though it was now after two o'clock. It was a pleasant day so I took lunch into the garden and after we'd eaten, I resolved that I would then take him inside and tell him all.

His mood was good, he seemed happier than of late and was coming up with ideas for the garden. It was only quite small and we had done as much as I thought we could with it really. We'd put a nice shrub border to one side and lots of pots down the other with an array of different plants and flowers. At the bottom, we had planted a beautiful white magnolia tree, looking healthy and growing taller year by year.

We ate lunch and I had started to feel much more relaxed. I'd decided not to tell him now and spoil his mood. I thought I would just leave it for that evening as I was quite enjoying seeing his happier side.

I cleared away the plates and cups then put them in the dishwasher and joined him once again outside. I wanted to keep busy myself so I started sweeping up the grass cuttings from the path, turning the soil along the shrubbery border and then I neatened the edge of the lawn with the spade. I didn't get to do the weeding in and around the pots but I could do that the following afternoon, as I would be at home. Nonetheless, it had been a good job done, and the garden was looking much tidier now. We'd worked hard and it showed.

Evening came and we were sat together watching TV, the tiredness of a late night the night before catching up with me, along with the gardening and fresh air. Paul's good mood was not so apparent and I assumed he was tired as well. I decided that I couldn't tell him then; it wouldn't have been fair to drop it on him late at night, followed by another sleepless night and an early start for work for him. I knew I couldn't keep putting it off like this and had to tell as soon as he got back in midweek. I knew it would be as much a shock for Paul as it had been for me … and still was.

# CHAPTER FORTY

I was off work for a few days so got up a little later than usual. Paul had left at his normal time. I started my housework early, as I wanted to go into Poole on the train, do a bit of shopping, and then get back to do the last jobs in the garden and scrub the patio. It was another nice morning so if I left and got back early enough I would be able to sit and have lunch in the garden again.

I was mopping the kitchen floor when the phone rang. I wasn't going to answer it as I didn't want to miss my train and still had yet to shower and have some breakfast. As the ringing continued, I worried whether it might be urgent or if there was a problem, especially it was still quite early, so I decided to answer it.

"Hello it's me, Mark. Please don't hang up." I froze momentarily to the spot. "I need to speak with you, Sue," I heard faintly, the phone held away from my ear, just about to hang up.

"I don't think we have anything to say, Mark, please can you just leave it."

He sounded desperate. "I haven't slept at all and I really am going out of my mind. I meant what I said, every word of it, Sue. *Please* can we talk about this face to face not on the phone?" he pleaded.

"No we can't!" I replied. "There is nothing to say. I have a husband and a beautiful daughter, and you have two children and a wife." Despite my mixed feelings towards her, she was still his wife.

I stood in silence for what seemed an eternity; I didn't want to speak with him, but then again, maybe I should hear what he was desperate to say to me. I was confused and didn't know how to deal with any of this; it had been so unexpected. I eventually answered him. "Mark, this is just wrong. I barely know what day is. You haven't slept and you think I have! I don't want to discuss this now. I have plans today and I'm going out but I will talk to you on the phone. You can say what you have to say to me and that will be the end of it." I hung up and my thoughts turned to Paul and Sarah. I couldn't think of anything but them.

I somehow finished my jobs got ready and left for my train, just making it with seconds to spare. They do run quite frequently but I had planned my day and this one was ideal timing. I sat down in the carriage which and planned where I wanted to go and tried to write a list. I thought about Mark's call and began feeling so guilty that my mind was in a complete whirl and my concentration evaporated.

Oh, Lord! I felt so uncomfortable and I hadn't even done anything wrong. I had only spoken to him for goodness sake. This was a horrible situation he'd caused, but I couldn't help but feel for him, too; he was a lovely friend. For him to suddenly open up to me in that way must have taken some doing. The more I thought about it, the more I thought that he must really mean it. What if he really was in love with me ... and why me? The more I thought of it the worse it all became.

I tried hard to clear it from my mind. I wanted to enjoy my day off and I was determined I was going to do just that. What better way to do it than a spot of retail therapy? I stuck to my list and bought the few things I'd wanted and had a walk along the quayside in Poole harbour, watching the boats passing by. Suddenly, I don't know why, but I remembered the boat I'd seen when I was younger, when I was on the bus to Walney Island and the bridge had been up to allow the boat though. I could still see that pretty lady sipping champagne on deck and the man who had smiled so beautifully at her. It was all just as clear as if it were yesterday.

I slowly ambled my way back to the station and went home. I had enjoyed my morning very much and it had been a successful trip. I made a sandwich and took it in the garden as I wanted to make the most of the fine weather. My pots were the next job on the list. I had bought a few new plants whilst I was out so I planted them, making an instant transformation. I was very pleased. What a difference a touch of colour makes to a garden; it was all looking very neat and tidy.

Paul was away until Wednesday, as usual, so I busied myself with various jobs around the house, just a bit of decorating, and a bit of a spring clean. The day flew by and by 9.30 that evening I was off to my bed, feeling that I'd enjoyed a productive day. I thought I'd read for a little while, but every once in a while, thoughts of Mark crept into my mind. I tried to block them out and didn't want another restless night so decided to turn out the light and go to sleep.

I slept right through; I couldn't remember the last time I had done that. I woke feeling really refreshed and ready for the day ahead. I had nothing especially planned, which was nice. I thought I'd listen to some music whilst doing a few jobs and then maybe pop down to Weymouth on the train for a walk on the beach and some sea air. I hadn't been for a while; I'm not overly fond of the place but once in a while I like to go. The beach is nice and if the weather stayed fine I thought I might even have lunch on the sand so prepared a packed lunch to take with me.

I put all my ironing away to 'Always On My Mind', still enjoying my Pet Shop Boys CD. I'd always liked them; they're in my top ten and I proudly have all of their albums. I'd always thought I'd like to see them one day. I'd heard they were rather boring live, but I'd still like to see them, I thought.

I went into the kitchen to put away the iron when the phone rang. I'd been expecting a call from work. "Hi!" I answered cheerfully. It was Mark. "Oh, hello … I was expecting a call from work." I felt guilty for sounding so chirpy. There was a bit of a silence before he spoke again.

"Can I please see you so we can talk about this?"

"No, Mark. We can talk now on the phone."

"Sue, I really don't want to have this personal conversation on the phone. I need to see you to explain and I'd like it to be today please. I have some time off. Is that OK?"

After a slight hesitation, I said "I don't think that's a good idea. I'm going to Weymouth anyway today and I really think you need to forget this, Mark."

"I can't forget it, Sue. I will pick you up and take you to Weymouth," he said "and we can talk in the car. Where shall I pick you up and what time?" He was not going to be put off again, I could tell.

"Pick me up in one hour," I relented. We agreed a meeting place. "We can talk on the way and I'll listen to what you have to say, that's all."

"Thank you, Sue, I'll be there." He sounded relieved. I wasn't! I wasn't happy about this at all but I had to hear what he wanted so desperately say to me.

He was already waiting at the meeting place as I turned the corner. He looked terribly nervous, sitting there deep in thought. He smiled brightly when he saw me, a smile that reminded me so much of the man on the boat. He opened the car door for me and I climbed in. Normally we would kiss each other when we were all together but that just didn't seem at all appropriate now.

"Thank you for agreeing to see me. I really appreciate it," he said as we drove off.

"Mark, I *cannot* believe I am here come on, let me hear what you have to say!" I demanded.

We waited. He really looked very nervous. I'd never seen him like this at all before; he was always so, confident, calm and relaxed. Not then he wasn't.

After a few moments where he seemed to be composing himself, he began. "I truly meant what I said to you, Sue. My heart has wanted to say it for a very long time." He pulled over, stopped the car and turned off the engine before turning towards me. "I am in love with you. I'm sorry but I'm so madly in love and I just had to tell you. I know it must be a shock and I've tried so many times to say it before, but just couldn't find the right time. I just seized what seemed like the right moment on Saturday night." He reached for my hand but I pulled away, He then continued to pour out his heart about his feelings how long ago they'd started. He talked about a cricket match when he'd first seen me picking

264

mushrooms in the outfield best part of twenty years ago at Kingston Maurward, and how he couldn't take his eyes off me even then.

I felt rooted to the seat, sitting perfectly still, taking in every word as it left his lips, every gesture and expression on his face. I saw tears welling in his eyes as he apologised over and over for feeling the way he did.

I knew then without any doubt at all, I could feel it in my heart: this was for real. It hadn't been a casual passing statement, or a silly flight of fantasy. He was in love with me. It isn't easy to explain how, but I knew he meant every single word. He then asked how I felt now I knew … and how I felt about him.

I sat very quiet for a while thinking about it his questions. I admired his honesty, but what were we to do now? I admitted to myself that I liked him very much; he was such a lovely, interesting person and, I thought, a very handsome man. I remembered when we'd first met noticing how we seemed to instantly gel. He always seemed so easy-going, like a breath of fresh air. I'd always felt so relaxed in his company and thought I knew him well, but I hadn't seen this coming at all.

"Sue, are you going to say anything?" he asked nervously.

"I am not quite sure what to say to be totally honest, Mark" I started, "but let me start by saying I am more than a little shocked that you feel like this and to the extent you obviously do." My mind seemed to be fast-forwarding all the times we'd been together, his little gestures and looks towards me and the compliments he'd always paid whenever he saw me. It was all adding up … it was so obvious now … I must have been either stupid or naïve not to have noticed before.

"Are you cross with me?" he asked.

"No, I'm not cross; I just can't believe how stupid I am not to have seen this coming." Maybe I had done deep down, but had chosen to ignore it? I really did like him and somehow his open and honest explanation had made me realise perhaps just how much. I said that I did have feelings for him.

What on earth do we do now I thought? We had to stop seeing each other, I told him, and no more socialising with him and Jo. We both must make up excuses and decline invitations when asked by either party. No more calls and in time this will hopefully fade away. We had to think of our families – I couldn't even imagine the ramifications there if we continued.

He was stunned and said that I was now being naïve and that doing what I'd suggested wouldn't stop his or my feelings. I just couldn't see any other option. The mere thought of having an affair was abhorrent to me and that was the obvious next step if it wasn't stopped immediately.

I couldn't go into Weymouth now all I wanted was to go home, close the door and lock myself in.

"Can you take me back please?" I asked. "I have some thinking to do and I need to be left alone to do that. Thank you for your honesty. I appreciate how hard this must have been for you, as this is one hell of an announcement. Part of me wishes you'd kept it to yourself, but then part of me is so glad you've told me."

The drive back was quiet. We both tried to change the subject but couldn't avoid it completely. We arrived back and I said goodbye, my eyes now stinging with tears. I climbed out of the car and made my way to the house, not looking back as I didn't want to see his face.

Instead, I remembered how he'd looked when I'd arrived earlier, wearing his beautiful smile. That's how I wanted to remember him.

I went inside, closed the door and locked it. I wouldn't be going anywhere now; I had so much on my mind. I went up to the lounge, sat bewildered and gave in to the tears. I knew we couldn't see each other anymore.

The next I knew it was two o'clock and I realised I had cried myself to sleep. I'd woken with a dreadful headache so went down to the kitchen and took some painkillers. I hadn't had a cup of tea since just after nine when I'd been ironing. I was so thirsty so I drank a pint of cold water with ice straight down and then decided to run a bath. I couldn't possibly go outside; my eyes were like 'pee-holes' in the snow, and that was being kind. I couldn't eat anything. I tried the sandwich I'd made earlier but began to retch immediately so threw my picnic in the bin virtually untouched.

I lay submerged in a mass of Sanctuary bubbles; the fragrance was lovely and with music gently playing in the background I tried to relax. I was trying so hard to distract myself and prevent thoughts of Mark from creeping into my mind, but I just couldn't, no matter how I tried. I kept seeing his face smiling at me. I went over and over what we'd talked about, long enough for the bath water to go cold.

I dried and dressed and went into the kitchen to prepare my tea. I was having chicken stir-fry and I began to prepare the meat. I just couldn't do it, though, no matter how hard I tried; there were far more important things on my mind than food. I decided to go up and begin the mammoth task of sorting my wardrobes. That would give me plenty of distraction as they were a complete mess and my shoes seemed to have taken over – I'm sure they multiply when I'm not looking. I'd been threatening to do this for ages and now was the perfect time.

It took me almost three hours, pairing my one hundred and twenty-four pairs of shoes (and counting), before putting all my dresses in colour order, from light to dark and then in descending length (sad, I know, but I do love it when it's done). What a difference. I had a bag full for the charity shop, too, so that was a good turn; as they say, one man's trash is another one's treasure.

Yes, it was all just a distraction, trying to do something 'normal', but after such a difficult day it helped.

# CHAPTER FORTY-ONE

Paul would be coming home again tonight and I knew I should do the right thing and tell him what had happened, but I also knew that I couldn't. I didn't know how I'd cope with the fallout. I went through all the scenarios in my mind and try as I might I simply couldn't work out how I was going to broach the subject. What was making it even worse was I was starting to realise how I felt about Mark. That was a bigger worry.

Paul came home but I remained silent about Mark's announcement and settled down for what would hopefully be a nice weekend together, nothing planned. On the Saturday, we set out for a little run in the car, but I didn't know where I wanted to go, so I suggested that we point the car in any direction and just see where we ended up. He said he was not going to drive aimlessly and wasn't even that bothered about going out so we went back home again. I suggested going out for a meal but he didn't want to do that so I cooked dinner. He seemed rather lethargic but as usual insisted he was Ok.

Nothing really happened over the weekend and before we knew it Monday morning had arrived and poor Paul was off again to work. I left the house at my usual time and was walking to work along the avenue of sycamores in Culliford Road when suddenly Mark appeared from behind a tree. He gave me such a fright.

"I hoped I would see you, but wasn't sure which way you walked. I just had to see you again, Sue, I just can't get you out of my mind." I was admittedly very happy to see him, too; my heart was pounding and I felt like almost childlike. I couldn't remember *ever* feeling quite like this, not ever. Over the last few days, the more I'd thought about him the more I'd realised that I was in love with him. I suppose I'd been blocking it out, suppressing my feeling, knowing that it was just so wrong.

You won't be surprised to learn that things developed from there. I shall now get straight to the difficult part, as I don't wish to prolong what you may already have suspected. We did end up having a love affair, albeit a fairly short one as we were discovered by a simple text message, which Mark had sent to me. Neither of us is proud of it, particularly the hurt that ensued for all concerned, but be assured that it was not done lightly. Yes, we know of all the clichés believe me, we've heard them all. All I can say is that we really were very much in love with each other.

Everyone is entitled to his or her opinions and I neither want, nor expect any kind of sympathy whatsoever. We deserved a lot of the pain that we endured thereafter and really didn't set out to hurt our families. We lost a few friends along the way, (but then were they real friends anyway?). Our best friends tried not to take sides. No-one knows what's around the corner for any of us at any time and until you are in such situations you don't know how it really is or what it feels like. Some people are often quick to judge and I do not wish to make light of what we did because it had many tragic consequences for those around us and for the two us. People you had hoped you could count on sometimes weren't there for you, but others provided support that hadn't been expected.

As painful and difficult as it was, I left my first sweetheart, the man I had loved for thirty-two years and to whom I'd been married for twenty-eight. Paul gave me our beautiful daughter, Sarah Jane who I am so very proud of and adore to the moon and back; and for her I shall always thank him. We'd raised Sarah proudly together and in her we will always have a connection; one day we may be grandparents to her children, and we will both love them equally I know.

Paul and I had so many happy years together, along with such memories to cherish forever and no-one can ever take them away. My decision was probably the hardest I've ever made. However, the man I divorced was not the man I married. I sought guidance from a marriage councillor whom I saw privately. I sat with her, opened my heart and truthfully told her everything, even more than I've been able to share here. She helped me to work out for myself whatever it was I needed to do. Leaving Paul has proved unquestionably to be have been the right decision for me.

# CHAPTER FORTY-TWO

Things between Mark and I moved on apace. They say that you don't know someone until you've lived with them, and I'd definitely thought a great deal on this, not to mention lots of warnings from well-meaning people. It was never really a concern; I just knew in my heart that he was right for me.

We needed a place to live now so Mark and I moved temporarily into a rented flat at the other end of town. It was conveniently placed for work and was brand new and very nicely finished. As a top-floor flat, it had commanding views over Dorchester and the surrounding countryside. It may not have been what we would ideally like to live in, but it was ours, our shelter from the world.

That world was very ugly for a while, with both our divorces underway within a few months. Mark had also started a new job, which was hard enough, let alone the understandably messy relationships we both had with our former spouses. Despite all this, being with Mark was so easy. I hadn't felt so relaxed and at ease in a very long time. We knew we couldn't let the divorces and everything surrounding the breakdown of two families get in between us. We learned to deal with everyone, however hard, and take in our stride and never did we let that world damage us. We both remained strong and positive throughout, as painful as it was at times;

together we could face anything that was thrown at us, and, believe me, so much was but I also think it possibly made us even stronger somehow.

After a few weeks, we decided to book a holiday and get away together, to properly spend time away from everything and to be alone. He took me to Turkey, a place I had always longed to visit. I was not disappointed with it at all, neither of us were. Turkey is a beautiful place with outstanding scenery and perfect weather. We really had a most wonderful time, and yes, the problems were of course going to be there when we returned home, but the break had helped us to handle it all a little better.

Within six months, as our rental period ended, we had found a lovely house on Poundbury in Dorchester and moved in the March. We enjoyed gradually furnishing it together and making it our first real home. I didn't feel it right to have too many things from the past surrounding us and so I decided to leave most of it all behind. It was a very gradual but most enjoyable process getting everything together that we'd need in our new life together. Even doing this with Mark was so easy; we chose everything together, from the dinner service to the furniture.

One obvious and desperately regrettable outcome of our action was that the build-up to Sarah's wedding was far from that which Sarah and I had hoped for. I shall never forget that awful day when Paul and I had to break the news to Sarah.

The weekend of the wedding had arrived and both divorces were through. I knew it would be hard for everyone, especially Sarah and Paul, but I knew we had to remain calm and mature on the day for Sarah and

Mark (the groom's) sake. The night before the wedding the family got together for a meal at a local restaurant. It was the first time Paul and I had met since the divorce. The event passed without incident.

On the morning of the wedding, Sarah, Paul and his mum were all together at a local guesthouse to get ready together. Unfortunately, there had been a mistake with the trousers of Paul's morning suit. They were *way* too short when he tried them on; he has a 33" inside-leg measurement and these must have been 29." I stood in his room, stifling a laugh, but remaining calm, I said obviously he couldn't possibly walk her up the aisle in them. The guests would think they'd arrived at a circus rather than a wedding. I was trying to make light of the situation; it wasn't Paul's fault; he'd been given them by the hire company and handed to him in a bag. Thankfully, the crisis was averted as they were taken back and replaced immediately.

I know it was far from the day Sarah dreamed of – nor was it for me – but her father and I sat in our rightful place together at the top table. She did have a fabulous wedding, the one all along I had been determined that she should. After the dreadful rain during the previous day and night, the day was filled with gloriously autumnal October sunshine. Most of all, Sarah was quite the most beautiful bride. I was so very proud of my baby.

I remember Paul telling me from the day I left him that he was terrified of being alone. One of the things he said to me was he didn't want to be on his own, whilst on his knees begging me to stay. I felt sure that he would find someone and I told him so, and believed that he whomever he met would be financially stable.

Hard as it may be to believe I still do really care about him; I know I left him but you can't erase those feelings, especially being together so long. He tried to get me to go back to him, saying all the things I'd been waiting to hear for so long, too long really. It was all sadly too late and seemed then out of character. Hindsight tells me we married too young but that's how it was back then. It was the first serious relationship either of us had had.

After I'd left but whilst we were still sorting out arrangements with the house and belongings we did keep in touch. I'd even offered to help him look for potential new partners whilst he was browsing various online dating sites. He was communicating with a couple of women regularly at the time, trying to work out next steps. I was so pleased when I heard a few weeks later that he'd actually met someone. Before too long their relationship had developed and I soon learned they were to marry very soon after.

Life for Mark and I now had started to calm down and we had settled beautifully into our new house. Christmas was fast approaching and we'd decided to get a real tree. We went out to a farm Mark knew and chose a freshly cut ten-foot-high spruce. It looked and smelled wonderful and I dressed it in silver from top to bottom. and the smell from it as you walked in the room was delightful. In a few days our few presents were arranged neatly underneath.

We had a lovely festive season and spent Christmas Day together. He'd bought me a pair of shoes, a dress and some perfume, none of which I'd known about beforehand. I was amazed and delighted at his impeccable choice and taste. It was lovely being in our own house after being in the flat last year. We saw a few friends over the holidays, some of whom had been there from the start and others who were gradually coming back as the dust had settled, and new ones we had made, too.

The New Year arrived and, as many people do, we used it as a time to plan what we needed and wanted to do around the house, in the garden and where we wanted to go for our holidays that year. We both very much enjoy our holidays; we have very similar tastes, whether enjoying the sunshine or sightseeing, which made choosing where to go always so easy. Mark said he really fancied going away to Dublin for a weekend break. It's a beautiful, vibrant place, with so much to see and do. I thought it was a great idea so I set about researching the options on the internet, which for me is always a pleasure in itself.

# CHAPTER FORTY-THREE

Dublin here we come! We set off for the flight from Bristol one Friday morning at the end of July in 2010. We were both very excited indeed and looking forward to a lovely weekend in the beautiful Irish capital. The flight was on time and we arrived mid-afternoon in bright, warm sunshine. The journey to the hotel didn't take long; the hotel was perfect and very handy for the city centre and close to the Temple Bar area. Once we'd unpacked, we went out to begin our sightseeing, then off to look for a traditional Irish pub that Mark had heard about, the Oliver St John Gogarty.

We soon found it in Temple Bar and went upstairs to find a table where we could sit and eat. There was a good programme of live music and we were soon encouraged by the toe-tapping group to sing along and join in with the jaunty Irish songs. What a tremendous atmosphere it was. I'd not experienced anything quite like it, nor seen and heard anyone at all like them; they were fabulous. We had a few drinks – Mark enjoying the Guinness – and a meal before deciding to move on and continue our obligatory Irish pub crawl. The streets were crammed with visitors like us and the pubs were so vibrant and exciting. They all had their own individual character and all bar none were filled to the rafters with revellers.

At midnight we made our way back to the hotel, by now very tired after an exciting and busy day. Saturday morning, we awoke early in our wonderful hotel room, got ourselves ready and went down for our delicious traditional Irish breakfast, where we finalised our plans for the day ahead. No time to waste as we were only here for the weekend, so off we set, straight from breakfast.

Our first stop was to see the Book of Kells at Trinity College, which we knew would be busy later in the day. In the queue through to the room where the book was displayed, through the old College library, I remember there being a large leather-bound book that was open on a particular page. We happened to stop and read the page, which was a journal report detailing how a man-eating tiger had killed a number of the British Army in India. For some reason, the illustrations and language used made rather an impression with me. We eventually filtered through to the darkened room with the illuminated display cabinets in which the Book was displayed. It was so much smaller than we'd expected, perhaps a little disappointing, but it was nonetheless worth seeing it.

From the College we went on to take in some of Dublin City sights on the open-topped bus. It was great being able to hop on and off as desired. One destination Mark, especially, wanted to visit was the Guinness Storehouse; we'd both seen it before some time ago but wanted to return. I saw so much I hadn't seen or remembered from the previous visit, including all the old Guinness memorabilia and TV adverts. If you've been, you'll know that at the end of the tour you can take the lift to the top of the tower, exchange a voucher for a pint of Guinness and enjoy the panoramic views over Dublin.

I don't actually like it myself but it's rude not to try and Mark, of course, gratefully enjoyed the remainder of my pint.

We'd already had a busy day, but that evening we were going out to a restaurant so we went back to the hotel for a rest. Mark had found the restaurant on line; it had fabulous reviews and, although we had a reservation, the restaurant was expected to be quite busy we needed to be punctual. Mark insisted that I needed to be ready for seven o'clock sharp to meet the taxi he'd arranged outside the hotel entrance.

I showered and got dressed in a beautiful new maxi dress, with high-heeled shoes and bag to match. Mark had gone down to reception whilst I finished getting ready then I went down to meet him in the hotel lobby promptly at seven o'clock as requested. He told me how beautiful I looked and kissed me gently. He, too, looked very smart in a new shirt and trousers. We stepped outside into the beautiful warm evening, the sun shining with just a few clouds in the sky. I turned to the taxi waiting by the hotel but Mark took my hand and led me in the opposite direction. We were walking towards a horse and carriage.

"That's our taxi!" he announced, beaming.

"*Really*? Oh, what a wonderful surprise. I've never been in one before. What a lovely idea." The coachman and proprietor, who I later learned was one Bernard Flannigan, climbed down from his seat, shook our hands and introduced himself. He was a dear little soul; a wiry and rather elderly man, but he looked very smart. Bernard proudly ushered us towards his perfectly groomed horse and immaculate carriage. Mark helped me climb aboard and then followed me before we both sat on the soft, thick, tan leather seats.

We were soon off on our journey. Bernard acted as a tour guide, pointing out places of interest along the way and telling us bits of history and trivia, which was lovely to hear, especially with his lilting Dublin accent. It started to rain gently so Bernard climbed down from his driver's seat and pulled the carriage roof across before setting off once more, leaving Mark and I in a little cocoon.

I vividly remember a gorgeous little dark-haired boy of about six or seven years standing at the corner of a street, holding his Mummy's hand while they waited to cross the road. When he saw the horse and carriage and then me peering out through the window, he gave a huge smile and he began waving at me. I waved back, which seemed to excite him even further as tugged at his Mummy's hand and with a huge grin pointed at our carriage.

I turned to show Mark who had been sitting on my left only to find him on one knee at my feet, looking rather nervous I might add. He took my hand and placed it in his left hand.

"Sue I am so in love with you. Would you do me the honour of marrying me?" In his right hand I then noticed an open box containing the most beautiful double diamond ring on a twist. I was totally taken aback. My mouth was open but I simply couldn't say a word. After a few moments (which Mark later said seemed like forever), he broke the silence.

"Are you going to answer me please? Is that a yes or a no?" and he smiled his beautiful smile.

Tears of joy were streaming down my face. Through the tears, I managed to tell him.

"Yes, I would be delighted to accept." Relieved, he sat down beside me again and kissed me. To say he was thrilled would be an understatement and I'd simply not seen this coming at all. I couldn't have ever dreamt of such a romantic proposal. It was simply perfect.

The shower had passed and the sun was now shining once more and we'd arrived at our destination, the Pearl Brasserie. Bernard climbed down and helped me from the carriage. I saw him whisper to Mark. The smile confirmed my response to Bernard who firmly shook Mark's hand, patted him on the back and congratulated us both. He had known all along what Mark had planned and seemed genuinely delighted that I had accepted.

We went inside and greeted by a lovely man who escorted us to the bar and gave us both a drink. We were shown to our table. It was a wonderful place, by far the nicest restaurant I had ever been in. I was floating above the clouds and permanently beaming the broadest of smiles; we were receiving glances and smiles from the other diners whom I imagined guessed what had happened. I didn't have much appetite really, as I was almost too excited to even think of food. However, I chose very well and the meal was exquisite, as was the service and atmosphere but especially my company. My fiancé had chosen impeccably.

During the meal, we chatted endlessly about the day and of course about the proposal. I learned that Mark had been very nervous about asking me, and that he had almost given away the surprise even before we'd left home when he'd asked me to put something else in his suitcase when he suddenly remembered the ring was inside. He had come bounding upstairs, telling me not to bother after all. I was so glad I hadn't discovered it as it would have spoiled the moment and all the work he had clearly put into it.

After slowly finishing our engagement meal we made our way back to the hotel and into the bar for a nightcap. We sat at the bar and got chatting to a lovely couple sitting next to us. During the conversation, they asked why we were in Dublin and I then told them about the proposal. The guy immediately and without hesitation clicked his fingers at the barman (not a gesture for which I generally approve!) and ordered a bottle of Möet and four champagne flutes. We were taken aback but very appreciative of the kind gesture. They had half a glass each, congratulated us once more and left us to enjoy the rest of it alone. What a thoughtful and generous thing for a complete stranger to do.

We sipped our last glass then retired to bed after what had been an eventful, most exciting day and romantic day. I still couldn't believe it; I kept looking at the beautiful ring on my finger to make sure that it really had happened. The smile had not left Mark's face.

We woke early, slightly thick-headed, and decided to take the train to Dun Laoghaire port and look around the place as it had been a recommendation from an Irish friend. So after breakfast we walked to the station and boarded the train. Mark turned and asked when I should like to get married and what sort of ceremony. I knew he didn't want a long engagement and I felt the same; there didn't seem any reason to wait, but I did know that I wanted to get married in church if it were possible, but I thought it not quite so easy to have a second marriage in certain churches. He was delighted as he wanted a church wedding himself but would be happy to do whatever I wanted.

Church wedding decided, we both said, at almost the same instant, (something we often do) that Stinsford Church, just outside Dorchester, would be a wonderful place to hold it. We laughed; of all the churches to choose we'd said the same one at the same time. So the decision had been made with regards to which church, as long as it was possible for us. It is a delightful church, and in its churchyard can be found the grave containing the heart of the novelist and poet Thomas Hardy. His ashes are buried in Westminster Abbey.

The next thing to decide was when we should get married. I knew I didn't want a winter wedding and thought June would be the perfect month for it. Mark instantly agreed, so June next year, in 2011, it would be. Neither of us wanted a big wedding, just our closest family and friends to share our special day. Mark said he would make some enquiries with the church and speak with the vicar once we got back home from Dublin.

We arrived at Dun Laoghaire and got off the train. The sun was shining and it was by now very warm. We walked along the water's edge and up and down the streets. It was a lovely place, what I remember of it as we were busy talking about our future wedding plans. Lunchtime was beckoning, so we found a lovely traditional pub with friendly staff and ate a light meal.

It was soon time to head back to the hotel and prepare to leave this fair city; we arrived at the hotel, collected our luggage from the reception and headed for the airport. We were having such a wonderful time, and the excitement of Mark's unexpected romantic proposal had made it even more special. The memories of that weekend will live with me forever. He is just so easy to be with and I have to admit I hadn't felt so relaxed and this happy for a very long time.

# CHAPTER FORTY-FOUR

We arrived back home to slightly cooler weather but at least it was dry. I was still on a high and would be for some time yet. We unpacked and settled down to enjoy what was left of a busy weekend.

On Monday morning, we were both back to work and I couldn't wait to share my news; everyone was very pleased for us as they all knew how difficult things had been and had been there to support me throughout. After I'd finished at work I went back home, quickly had some lunch, put my wedding planning head on and began making lists of all the things that needed to be done. I was so excited and in the zone now, with all sorts of ideas and details springing into my head. I was determined to enjoy the pleasure of planning this day. I knew that Mark would be happy with whatever I wanted, but we would do it together. So I just jotted a few things down and put them aside to go through with him.

Mid-afternoon he called me as he does every day and said he had been enquiring as to who the vicar of Stinsford church was. *She* was the Reverend Janet Smith. He'd already tried to call her at lunchtime but she hadn't been available. Sounding a little disappointed, he said he would try again when he came home unless I wanted to try later.

I'd finished what I'd been writing on my list and thought I would try to call her myself and fortunately was successful. She was a delightful lady, most friendly and understanding of our situation. She promptly invited us for tea and a chat, so that Friday afternoon we went to see her. Right from opening the door she made us feel so welcome and at home. We talked in turn about ourselves and our situation and she asked us both to write a little page for her outlining our reasons for wanting to be married, which we could talk through at the next meeting.

She found her diary and asked us which date we were considering. I'd already discussed with Mark that I should like a Friday and we had earmarked the third of June. We suggested the date and she said that it was free and proceeded to write it in her diary for us. We were delighted and a little surprised at how well it had all gone with her.

We now had our date and it was less than a year away. We still had plenty to arrange and plan but we were going to do it at a leisurely pace, enjoying every step. Simple but tasteful was the order of the day. Luckily, everything we chose fell into place without any problems at all. The only thing we weren't going to be able to organise was the weather; I just prayed it would at least be dry but a bit of sunshine would be lovely, if only as we left the church for the photographs.

I had decided to ask our very good friend, Paul, to walk me down the aisle, which we did when the four of us went out for a meal. He immediately and rather proudly agreed. We also I asked his partner, Gloria, to be my matron of honour, to which she too happily agreed.

We chose was The Kings Arms in Dorchester as the venue for the reception. It was a lovely old coaching inn, local and very handy for our guests, with an upstairs function room perfect for what we had in mind. Steve, the manager, was super in helping us decide on all the details, offering great advice and generally reassuring us that all would be perfect on the day. He unexpectedly suggested that we could serve champagne in the picturesque churchyard after the ceremony, as long as the vicar approved. He said the guests would welcome this while the wedding party was busy with all the photographs. What a splendid idea!

For the reception, we wanted a simple traditional roast dinner (salmon for the vegetarians) and a choice of puddings, with a Mezze starter. Everything was agreed and accepted without fuss and all done in one visit. We also had an evening reception and dance to follow immediately from the wedding breakfast. Steve also offered us the beautiful bridal suite for the night and on viewing it we snapped up the kind offer. We couldn't refuse the huge, beautifully furnished room, four poster bed set resplendently within, and a wonderful bathroom.

The flowers I chose were to be my favourite, white Lilies. I wanted them everywhere possible, and my great friend Nicky kindly offered to arrange them for us as a wedding present along with beautiful table decorations, and pew end flowers. It was so kind of her. She is so artistic and talented and I knew she would do us proud.

Finally, we chose the order of service, hymns and readings together, not to mention, of course, the music for my bridal march and our departure, as man and wife, at the end of the service. It was fun listening to lots of different hymns and pieces of music. Mark even designed and printed the order of service books. We had a lovely engagement period and both enjoyed planning, choosing and preparing everything for our day together.

Once all was sorted we went on holiday for a week to Ibiza, where I'd found a late deal, and I have to say I was most surprised at how beautiful it was. I'd done my research prior to booking and knew where to avoid, given all the clubbing reviews and reports you hear, but I'd chosen a resort on the picturesque side, at the top of a rocky cliff with a beautiful sandy beach far below.

The time flew by and before we knew it was time for our hen and stag weekends, which we'd decided to have on the same weekend. I went to Windsor for an overnight stay with my girlfriends and had a super time; it was a beautiful day, sipping champagne around a fountain and eating fairy cakes when we arrived, whilst waiting for our rooms to be made up. A former private school, the hotel had wonderful ground and buildings; Mark and I had previously stayed there and enjoyed it so I knew what to expect. Windsor is also a beautiful town, dominated by the famous castle looming over it. It was a good choice for the occasion and Gloria kindly planned and arranged it all.

Mark had arranged to stay in Dorset and go clay pigeon shooting and then onto quad biking at the same venue with a posse of friends before heading on the train into Weymouth for an evening pub crawl.

Gloria and I shared a twin room in our hotel and were getting ready for the evening when her partner Paul rang. I was getting dressed when I heard her say "Oh dear, shall I tell Sue?" I looked across at her and she was looking rather worried. Once she'd hung up I asked what was wrong.

"Oh, it's Mark. I'm afraid there's been an accident …" I froze to the spot. I began to tremble and sat on the bed, feeling the colour drain. The last thing I'd said as I kissed him goodbye was to take care we don't want any accidents. "He's is OK, but maybe a little concussed," she said. Oh my God what had happened? She went on to tell me that he had lost control of the quad bike; the ground was so dry and the clouds of dust had meant he couldn't see where he was going and had hit a tree whilst following everyone back to the garages. Me being me, I imagined the worst.

The girls were starting to arrive at our room for a pre-meal drink and a few of them had been informed and updated on Mark's condition. I was assured he was OK, that he was suffering a sore head and a few cuts and bruises, but that he was not in any serious condition at all. He did phone me as he knew I would have been informed and would be worried, but my mind was now put to rest. We all then went out and enjoyed a lovely evening but my mind was frequently with Mark.

We left the hotel after breakfast the next day and walked around Windsor, sat in the park by the Thames to have an ice-cream, undertook a bit of retail therapy before heading home. I couldn't wait to see Mark; despite reassurances, I had still been worried. I arrived home just after five o'clock. He heard me coming toward the house across the gravel and opened the door. He was so pleased to see me and I immediately could tell he wasn't quite right. He was limping and hugged me rather gingerly. He showed me the cuts and scratches on his legs and when he showed me the ruined jeans he'd been wearing it looked like he'd been attacked by a some huge clawed beast; when thrown off the quad-bike he'd landed in a thorny-hedge before his head hit a tree, thankfully protected by a helmet.

He was limping and his neck was a bit stiff. I suggested seeing a doctor or even going to the hospital but he really didn't feel it necessary. I insisted that if he felt no better the next day he must see the doctor. I shall never understand what it is with men and seeing anyone medical!

Fortunately, he was feeling much better the next day and he seemed to be moving easier, the bruising was coming out, but I was happy he was on the mend, and am delighted to say he continued to make a full recovery before the wedding!

# CHAPTER FORTY-FIVE

I awoke on Friday June 3rd, 2011 at ten past seven in the morning. Today was the day I was to marry my beloved Mark and I was *so* excited. As I drew back the curtains the sun was pouring through the window; it was just what we'd hoped and prayed for but knew that the wedding was not for another eight hours so kept my fingers crossed.

Mark had gone to stay with his friends, Pete and Cathryn overnight, as per tradition so as not to see the bride on the day before the church. He sent me a beautiful text first thing making my heart race even more. I'd left Mark a note to open on the morning. My sister, Diane, Alan and Mark were with me, having arrived a few days earlier to kindly help with the last-minute preparations. Alan had previously thoughtfully offered to chauffeur Paul and I to the wedding in Diane's beautiful silver Volvo convertible, and then take Mark and I from the church to the reception after the service. We were all staying at the King's Arms, along with a number of our guests.

We all got up and had breakfast, not that I was very hungry. I was far too excited to think about food but Diane encouraged me to eat something as it was going to be a long day. Nicky came to take me to the church to put the flowers out with her, as I'd known she would;

she did a truly professional job and the arrangements in the church were breathtaking.

I went back home and the pre-wedding pampering began. Steve, the manager at the King's Arms, had suggested that we (me, Diane and Gloria) should get ready in our hotel room, so off we set, armed with chilled champagne. Emma, my amazing hairdresser and long-time friend would be arriving soon at the hotel.

Mark had sent me the most beautiful mixed bouquet to the hotel and it was sitting on the table in our room as I arrived, with a beautiful message inside.

We had such a lovely time getting ready together and without really noticing the time, Paul shouted into to room to see if we were ready. Where had the time gone? Suddenly the butterflies started. Alan was outside, standing by the car and looking very smart. The sun was thankfully still shining and was now very warm. I really couldn't believe how beautiful the weather was; it couldn't have been better.

I stepped out of the room, carefully walked down the steps holding the hem of my long beautiful ivory dress, and was helped into the car. We then set off for the church which wasn't far, so Alan drove steadily as I wanted to enjoy every second of the day (and because the roof was down!). Diane and Alan had dressed the car with more white lilies, streaming beautifully across the dashboard and behind me on the shelf. I could smell their delicate fragrance as the breeze gently played with them.

We arrived at the church and I saw Gloria outside the church with the vicar. I was helped out of the car, I thanked and hugged Alan and he went inside. Paul took my hand, I linked his arm, and we started to walk along the path towards the church door. I began to feel slightly nervous; he looked at me and asked if I was OK. I said I was very excited, but just a little nervous. He was so calm and reassuring and said we would stop outside, take a breath and wait until you feel ready. After a few moments and some giggling, (which I later found out had announced my presence to Mark and the guests inside) we looked at each other and stepped towards the church, where we were met by Gloria and Janet, the vicar. I could hear the organ playing. Janet went into the church first, followed by Paul and I and then Gloria. I stopped to kiss Nicky who was at the back of the church and thanked her once more for the beautiful flowers as I could now appreciate the full effect.

I then saw my fiancé at the altar, looking so handsome and smiling that beautiful smile back at me. He looked so happy I thought he was about to burst. He immediately took my hand as I arrived at his side and kissed it, then turned to me saying how beautiful I looked and how much he loved me. I heard the door close and tip toes of feet entering the church and wondered who that might be.

The service was beautiful. We said our vows and exchanged rings; we sang our hymns lustily and said our prayers. By three twenty, we were husband and wife and it felt perfect. I was so proud of my boy. He had made me the happiest woman alive. And I know he was the happiest man. We had a few photographs of the signing of the registers before turning to walk, arm in arm, back down the aisle to be greeted by the smiles and grins on all our friends.

We left the church for more photographs whilst the guests sipped champagne in the beautiful sunshine. We discovered who the late arrivals were, tiptoeing into the church at the start, when Sarah and Russell from Derby came to apologise for their late entrance. They'd had a terrible journey down and were so delayed that they ended up having to stop in a church hall en-route to get dressed. Their story made us all roar with laughter at the thought of Sarah getting dressed in the ladies' toilet at Frampton village hall! Russ is Mark's best friend from university they go back a long way. A truly wonderful couple, well I should say family as they have two super boys, George and James (Mark's godson), all of whom we are very fond.

My husband passed me a glass of champagne and we had a little moment together in the shade of a tree. We were looking round at our family and guests, all dressed smartly, talking about our wonderful day, when he turned to me. "Thank you, darling, for making me the happiest man. I adore you and I'm so proud to be your husband. I will love you and look after you always."

We then circulated among our guests, all of whom commented on the service, the wonderful weather and the lovely setting. Alan Cottee came up to me, smiling, and told me that, aside from his own, this was the best wedding he'd been to and had not expected to be standing in the churchyard where Thomas Hardy's heart was buried, drinking champagne in the warm sunshine. At one point, he'd apparently looked down at the headstone nearest him and whispered "I bet you wish you were up here right now, because you're missing a great party." What a lovely thing to say. His words really touched me and meant a lot.

The whole day was perfect from beginning to end: the build-up, the service, the photographs, the food, the weather (which I later learned was to be the hottest day of the year) and the guests, more of whom were invited to join us in the evening for a dance and a light supper. For our first dance, and for a little bit of fun, Mark and I had choreographed a little jive routine. So the party started with Paolo Nutini's 'Pencil Full of Lead', which we executed to perfection, even in my dress. We had such fun dancing it and it brought smiles from all our guests, some of whom caught it on camera.

Midnight struck and it was time to say farewell to our guests, many of whom stayed up very late I understand, talking and drinking. We saw many of them the next morning at breakfast where we swapped stories and reminiscences from the day before. After saying all our farewells later that morning, we returned home to finish packing for our honeymoon.

# CHAPTER FORTY-SIX

Sunday morning came and we set off for our flight to Turkey from Bristol, another gorgeous day and easy journey as it was an early flight so there was no traffic. Mark had checked in online so it was all hassle free when we arrived. We boarded, took our seats with extra legroom and then once airborne a member of the cabin crew arrived with champagne that Mark had previously arranged. She announced our marriage to all the passengers and we were treated to a round of applause and congratulations.

We arrived at our destination and checked in to the magnificent new hotel. It did not disappoint at all; it was beautiful, with its own private beach, amazing views along the coastline and islands, several restaurants and bars and of course, the weather was simply perfect. Our room was high on the eighth floor. There was a wide-open view of the sea and the room itself was very tastefully decorated in creams and jade, ironically the same as at home. The maid had decorated the huge bed and the bathroom with deep red rose petals and, using one of the towels, she had made a swan, which sat it in the middle of the petals on our huge bed. It all looked so romantic.

It was the perfect week from start to end, going out for various trips to local towns, local temple ruins, and the like, before returning to relax around the pool or walk along the sandy shore. I really didn't want to come home at all, but then our lovely new home was waiting for us. We arrived back home on the twelfth of June to more lovely weather, Mark carried me across the threshold as we arrived at the front door and we were in our home now as Mr and Mrs Ashley and it felt truly wonderful.

We have now been married for almost four years and I can say in all honesty and from the bottom of my heart that I have never been so happy, or felt so loved and wanted, or felt so relaxed and at ease with someone. Life with my husband is so fulfilling in every way imaginable. We share so much and have many things in common; we laugh, really laugh together; we frequently finish each other's sentences, or say the same thing at the same time. It's a much-overused term but I truly have found my soul mate and I adore him the world over. He says exactly the same of me, and also that I am the most important thing in his life, and that my happiness is paramount to him.

In our time together, so far we have enjoyed so many things, little things as well as the big things. We've done Tango classes together (I love to dance); he booked me a helicopter flight for Christmas last year; we've enjoyed a balloon ride together over Bath; we've dune-buggied in Kos and in the deserts of Egypt, para-glided in the Aegean and swum in the Gulf of Mexico. Equally, we love just to walk the beaches and hills in Dorset, or find a quiet country pub. And we still leave each other little love notes.

Oh, and there's Australia. I haven't forgotten about Australia. I know I will get there this time.

My life is so happy and complete now. Leaving Paul was a very hard decision and I don't wish to make light of it at all. Neither do I want to sound selfish, but life is too short not to be happy. We only get one shot and it's no dress rehearsal, we all deserve happiness. Follow your heart. Things often happen for good reason and are meant to be and I now know that for certain.

I have shared lots of things in this book; and things I have learned about myself; many lessons and very personal experiences over the years, especially over the past decade, some particularly hard ones too I might add. I have lost family through death or greed and lost friends through my love for Mark. Important people are those who are now in my life who truly want to be there and for me to be happy and to share my happiness. What matters above all is Mark and my closest family.

Mark doesn't only tell me he loves me, but he also *shows* me that he loves me each and every day. One thing that he says often, "I loved you lots yesterday, and I love you a bit more today, but I know I shall love you even more tomorrow." And so I look forward to all my tomorrows, as I know they will be even better than today. Whenever I think life cannot possibly get any better, it just does.